Time

Looking Back At Life

5-15-19

"From Grandpa With Love"

Congratulations, Doug!
May God Bless You and the
Wichita Downtown Rotary Club
during your year as President!

Marion J. Martin

See Exp #3 v ans #70

A Collection of Later in Life Writings

"From Grandpa With Love"

Volume VI

There is a time for everything,
and a season for every activity under heaven...
He has made everything beautiful in its time.
(Ecclesiastes 3:1, 11a)

A Personal Note

What you are about to read is a series of insights God graciously gave me as He brought me from birth to old age. As you will see they were unfolded gradually as I traveled through life.

I never intended to write this book, but like all believers, I am called to be God's witness. In 2015, we completed the *From Grandpa With Love* books, consolidating many of the booklets I had written over the preceding 35 years. Within a few months, I felt God nudging me to begin a series of *One-Liners* accompanied by one page vignettes that had changed my life, (particularly after I stopped going My Way and started going God's Way) and email them to Family and Friends. When they were completed it seemed they, too, should be consolidated and placed in this book so they can better be passed on to those who are following.

In order to best understand the trip, I encourage you to think of life as a 24 hour day. Since the average life span is about 80 years, each 3 hours represents 10 years. So at 3:00 a.m., we are age 10. We are age 20 at 6:00 a.m., and sharp and ready for the day. But by noon we have suddenly reached mid-life, age 40! Now time begins to speed up. By 6:00 p.m. we realize we are 60 years old and thinking about retirement. By 9:00 p.m., we are age 70—it will soon be time to settle in and wait for the stroke of midnight.

Now comes the hard part: Each of us needs to ask, "Where am *I* on the clock, and what is *my* role at this season of life?" Because this is my account, I have divided these pages into the chapters God gave to me, and placed a clock and a short description of each era at the beginning of each section. At age 93, it is about 4:00 a.m. the Next Day and I am clearly in *Overtime*!

I hope my experiences will help, but each of you will need to see how God is directing *your* "Day". I found it is good to look back and learn from the Past. It is also good to look forward with hope and expectancy toward the Future. But I urge you to concentrate especially on Now, because it is the only time we have to be and to do. The rest are merely recollections and hopes.

Who we are and what we think and do changes as we go through life. I have concluded most young people start out thinking we will "fix" the world. But by the time we finish, we all know we didn't! Now I see that God didn't send us into the world to "fix" it, but rather to give us the opportunity to let Him "fix" us—if we only surrender our will and let Him use us to help make *"His kingdom come and His will be done, on earth as it is in Heaven."*

When we live the life Jesus proclaimed (as beautifully condensed in the Sermon on the Mount) we are fulfilled and the conditions in the world do often become better. But they do so as a result of following Him and letting Him use us, and not because we did it. As a result, God gets the Glory!

Since all Jesus' followers are called to be witnesses and the only first-hand account we have is our own, there are no perspectives in these stories but mine, except in a general way to give them a home. But I was truly blessed by everyone—family, friends, law associates and all the others who have contributed to my life.

Some of these *One-Liners* have appeared in earlier writings; others are simply recollections. Some are mirrors that reprove me and help me see inside myself; others are windows that give me a view outwardly that I have never seen before. Some are from talks, conversations, scriptures or other writings; others are from the Holy Spirit at critical times. Some I recall vividly; others are events which gradually crystallized into a sentence or two in my mind. And some are simply statements I have voiced as God drew me closer to Him over all these years.

But all have changed my life for the better—
And He, and everyone who has contributed, has my profound

Thanks!

Marvin J. Martin
Wichita, Kansas
2018

Contents

Part I

Going My Way
Age 0-44

Part II

Going God's Way
Age 44-On

Part I

Going My Way

Age 0-44

Life as a 24 Hour Day

Our "Day" begins at 12:01 a.m.
and
We Grow through the Wee Morning Hours

A Time To Be Born—And Grow Up
Age 0-16
(1925-1941)

3

Better to meet a bear robbed of her cubs

than a fool in his folly.

(Proverbs 17:12)

A Time To Be Born—And Grow Up

Age 0-16

#1 *"Never come between a mother bear and her cubs!"*

I still remember my 5th birthday in August, 1930. After lunch and blowing out the candles, we ate birthday cake, climbed into our car and headed out for Yellowstone National Park.

When we arrived at the Park entrance, Dad opened his bag and to my surprise, pulled out a small pistol—which the Ranger promptly plugged so it couldn't be fired. Later, we were all surprised, and frightened, when Dad walked toward some young bear cubs and was suddenly confronted by a huge, adult bear keeping guard!

That night the Ranger at the campfire made the lesson clear, when he told us, *"Never come between a mother bear and her cubs!"*

I learned two lessons I never forgot: Be very careful when you are in unfamiliar territory. And, be very careful not to come between *any* mother and her children!

There was one more, less obvious but perhaps more important lesson. Our parents were building us together as a family. No matter how hard the times, we seemed to get away most summers. Dad would pack a tent and luggage on one running board and in an extra trunk on the rear. We three boys would be in the backseat, with luggage between the seats, topped by our bedding. At times one of us saw a lot of the countryside, facing the window in enforced silence as "time out" for quarreling.

But we were together. And we were building memories that have lasted for a lifetime. Those vacations helped make us a family.

And families are *very* important for bears *and* boys!

From Grandpa With Love

It is better not to vow a vow
than to vow a vow and not fulfill it.
(Ecclesiastes 5:5)

A Time To Be Born—And Grow Up

Age 0-16

2 *"Who will take the pledge?"*

From age 7 to 12 (1932-1937) we lived on a little farm near Wichita. I attended a small two room (actually one room with a metal gate that was lowered into place except for special occasions) country school. One room was for grades 1-4, and the other for grades 5-8.

National Prohibition against alcohol had just been repealed. The Women's Christian Temperance Union (WCTU) was active. One day two ladies appeared in our school-room and talked about the evils of intoxicating liquor. It was dramatic! I remember, (at least I think I do) watching a worm dropped into a jar of alcohol where it shriveled and quickly died   When they asked, *"Who will take the pledge?"* never to drink intoxicants, I readily signed!

Later, I forgot the incident and drank socially, until my faith deepened, and I discovered Ecclesiastes 5:5 telling us it is better not to vow a vow than to vow a vow and not fulfill it.   So I stopped drinking alcohol.

Then I thought about all my vows: Boy Scout oath. Oath to join the military. Marriage vows. Church vows. Oath to practice law. The government even sought compliance for testimony and taxes under threat of perjury. It seemed everywhere I turned we were binding each other not based on our actions, but upon our oaths.

I decided it is better when I follow God voluntarily because I love Him and want to do His will—not because of oaths and vows.

From Grandpa With Love

Of what use is money in the hand of a fool,

since he has no desire to get wisdom?

(Proverbs 17:16)

A Time To Be Born—And Grow Up

Age 0-16

3 *"Save some, spend some, give some."*

My pay allowance for work done on our little farm was 25¢ a week. That doesn't sound like much, but it really wasn't so bad because 25¢ would buy two hamburgers (5¢ each), a "coke" (5¢) and a Saturday Movie Matinee (10¢). Along with the allowance came the admonition to **"Save some, spend some, give some"**.

Saving wasn't too hard. I still recall Dad opening an account for me with an initial $5.00. I enjoyed seeing the numbers slowly climb as I put away part of my 25¢ each week. But later I had to be careful not to fall in love with my bank account.

Spending then became a little too easy. I found myself about age 30 with nothing much in the bank. I decided never again!

Giving was the hardest since we were taught self-reliance. Gradually the Bible made it clear I was simply a receiver who was to enjoy, increase and then distribute the gifts entrusted to me.

As I look back now, I see **saving** was much better than debt. **Spending** brought a lot of pleasure. And **giving** to others helped us both.

Dad's little money-mantra was really about balance. When I learned to use moderation and **"Save some, spend some, give some"**, life became fuller and much richer. More beautiful and enjoyable—for me and for others!

Lord, thanks for Godly lessons our parents patiently poured into us over the years. Help us pass them on to those who follow us.

From Grandpa With Love

For the message of the cross is foolishness
to those who are perishing,
but to us who are being saved
it is the power of God.
(I Corinthians 1:18)

A Time To Be Born—And Grow Up

Age 0-16

4 *"The Old Rugged Cross"*

My mother was a 5'4" giant. Born into the family of a largely self-taught pastor father and homemaker mother, she grew up wearing left-over clothes from missionary barrels, and left home at age 16 to work in a bank. She played an enormous role in my life.

She clothed and fed us, taught us, nursed us when we were ill, helped get us get to church and encouraged us in everything we did. I suppose everyone has nostalgic childhood memories that affect us throughout life. One of mine, is our family gathered around an upright piano in the dining area of our old farm house during the depression years of the 1930's, as she played and we sang a few simple old hymns, including *"The Old Rugged Cross"*. The melody, words and memories are still strong 80 years later.

Mom was an encourager. Whatever we wanted to do, whether it was raising animals, buying a pony or later a car, singing on a radio Amateur Hour, or joining up to fly during WWII, she was enthusiastically for it!

She wanted us to live our own lives. To be released to reach for anything. Never overly protective, even when she watched me prepare to leave for overseas shortly after a memorial service for my oldest brother who was killed in an air crash over England.

The song she played was beautiful and the words are strong. But it is actually a memory hook that gives me a renewed thanksgiving for a mother who loved us enough to sacrifice all those years raising us, and then let us go to become men. What a gift!

From Grandpa With Love

Then the angel showed me the river of the water of life,
as clear as crystal,
flowing from the throne of God and of the Lamb
down the middle of the great street of the city.
(Revelation 22:1)

A Time To Be Born—And Grow Up

Age 0-16

5 *"Swim with the current!"*

I was about eleven years old, and attending a summer camp. I was about to have my own first-hand encounter with death.

Everything went well until Sunday afternoon. We were swimming in the river where they had dredged out the sand. Without realizing it, the current was taking us away from the sandbar where we had congregated. Suddenly it seemed the river was full of floundering, yelling boys who were trying to swim upstream and get back to the safety of the sandbar where we had been standing.

I still recall looking up and seeing a cloud and wondering if it was the last cloud I would ever see, and then hearing a voice call out from the bank, *"Swim with the current!"* After turning and going with the river, I could gradually move to the bank, and safety.

But one young camper did not make it. The next few days we heard them set off explosives trying to raise the drowned boy's body. The episode climaxed by us all attending his funeral.

The experience left me with a new sense of my own mortality and provided a myriad of lessons I have pondered and used many times during later years—including listening to others, not fighting against God's current in life, and the power of a simple statement.

I am eternally grateful to that man. I wish he could have attended our family reunion on my 90th Birthday last August and met all our children, grandchildren and great grandchildren he also saved!

From Grandpa With Love

13

Whatever you do, work at it with all your heart,
as working for the Lord, not for men,
since you know that you will receive an inheritance from the Lord
as a reward.

(Colossians 3:23-24)

A Time To Be Born—And Grow Up

Age 0-16

#6 *"Never work for anyone else."*

I wish you could have known my father, James Claude Martin, aka "J.C." He was born in 1877 and was 47 years old when I arrived. In a way he was a little like the grandfather figure I never knew. He lived in the age of personal responsibility and staunch individualism. He wanted the same for us, and encouraged us, *"Never work for anyone else."*

Dad grew up on a farm in Missouri and left home at age 14. He worked on a cattle ranch, traded properties, operated a funeral parlor after taking a two week course on embalming, owned a general store and ended up a Wichita builder.

Those were the days when there were home-owned shops and companies everywhere we walked. No giant international companies, or chain stores or franchises. The food and the products were vastly inferior to those we have today, but somehow the men who operated those little shops and companies often seemed much larger, even though their workplaces were smaller.

I enjoyed working independently, but the work world has changed. Today, most people work for someone else. The real challenge is to do our work *"with all your heart, as working for the Lord".*

The Bible says it is a gift of God to find satisfaction in our toil. For me, real satisfaction came when I *surrendered my independence and became dependent on God*, and **inter**dependent with others He is using to carry out His work!

From Grandpa With Love

Life as a 24 Hour Day

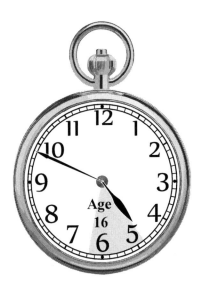

By Age 16 it is 4:48 a.m.
and
We Burst Awake into the World

A Time for War—and Peace
Age 16-21
(1941-1946)

Even youths grow tired and weary

and young men stumble and fall;

but those who hope in the Lord will renew their strength.

They will soar on wings like eagles;

they will run and not grow weary,

they will walk and not be faint"

(Isaiah 40:31)

A Time For War—And Peace

Age 16-21

7 *"Let me tell you how I learned to fly!"*

Because Wichita was a pioneer in building aircraft, it was perfectly positioned to play a major part in the war effort during the 1940's. The Army sent in a veteran flyer to act as liaison officer with the aircraft companies. One of his sons and I had become good friends, and we wanted to join the Aviation Cadet program. Since this required letters of recommendation, I suggested we ask his father to write for us.

When we approached the Colonel, he readily agreed, but added, *"Let me tell you how I learned to fly!"* As I remember the story, it was about 1913 and the air age was just beginning. He was placed in the cockpit of one of those early, single-seat aircraft you see in old pictures. His airfield was a pasture. After taxiing alone from one fence to another a few times, he was asked if he had the hang of it. When he agreed, the instructor said: "Take her off!"

I expect the loss ratio was high! Those of us who came later received the benefit of their trial and error. I'm sure many of us lived, because many of them didn't. It brought an entirely new respect for those early men who had the courage to solo without any flight instruction, and to fly those flimsy, early planes.

We all live on the fruit of the sacrifices of those who came before us.

This is a thank you letter to all those who paved the way for us!

From Grandpa With Love

The Lord said to him, "Who gave man his mouth?
Who makes him deaf or mute?
Who gives him sight or makes him blind?
Is it not I, the Lord?
Now go; I will help you speak
and will teach you what to say."

(Exodus 4:11-12)

A Time For War—And Peace

Age 16-21

8 *"You are a Navigator."*

I was 16 years old when World War II began in December, 1941. It was an Air dominated war. All many of us could think about was getting to fly. After two years of waiting and taking high-school courses to help prepare us, some of my friends and I left for Army Air Corps (as it was known in those days) training.

As Aviation Cadets, they tested us to determine whether we should be a Pilot, Navigator or Bombardier. My highest score was as a Navigator, who thinks and plans. My lowest passing score was as a Pilot, who is more interested in action and reaching the objective. I wanted to be a Pilot since that was the glory seat. They said, *"You are a Navigator."* I thought they were wrong.

But as the years rolled by, I came to the realization they were right. I learned I could fly an airplane, but I will never be a Pilot. Instead I have been a Navigator all my life, and functioned as a Navigator does, by determining where we are, where we want to go, and how we get there.

Chuck Swindoll, in his excellent book, *"Saying It Well"* encouragers us, *"Know who you are; Accept who you are; Be who you are."* It is hard enough to know who we are, but sometimes it is even harder to accept who we are.

Until I accept and become the person God has planned, I never fit. I know it, and so do others. Once I let go and become the person God designed, I enjoy me—and so do others.

From Grandpa With Love

A prudent man sees danger and take refuge,
but the simple keep going and suffer for it.
(Proverbs 22:3)

A Time For War—And Peace

Age 16-21

9 *"The point of no return!"*

As we trained for long distance flights during World War II, we learned there could come a point we had gone so far there was no turning back. They called it, *"The point of no return!"*

We thought about the issue flying over several thousand miles of ocean to reach our field on Guam, but arrived without incident. We had to sweat it out once, but we always had enough fuel for our B-29 to get back from our missions over Japan.

But take-offs were another matter! Trying to get off the ground with a full bomb load, and maximum fuel for a 3000-4000 mile flight, was a challenge. Our runway ended abruptly with a several hundred foot cliff that dropped down to the ocean. There was a *"point of no return"* on the runway where the pilot must either cut the engines and abort the mission, or totally commit to flight.

Planes left every minute. Sometimes we would watch as one took off, dropped out of sight to gain speed, and after several anxious moments, come back into view miles out at sea. If the pilot misjudged, they went over the cliff and crashed!

War-time has hectic, unusual difficulties, but it can provide some good life lessons. One is to be conscious of our own *"point of no return"*—whether it is a late yellow light at a street-corner, a risky relationship, or a dubious stock deal.

It's obviously smarter to stop in time, rather than ignoring the signal that we are about to go over a cliff and crash!

From Grandpa With Love

For I myself am a man under authority,

with soldiers under me.

I tell this one, "Go", and he goes;

and that one, "Come", and he comes.

I say to my servant, "Do this", and he does it.

(Matthew 8:9)

A Time For War—And Peace

Age 16-21

 # 10 "Yes Sir!" "No Sir!" "No Excuse, Sir!"

The Air Corps was not a democracy. Our enlistments were for the duration of the war, so we learned patience. We were taught early on to respond to those above us in rank with a pattern of, *"Yes Sir!" "No Sir!" "No Excuse, Sir!"*

We slept in unison, marched in unison, ate in unison, showered in unison, wore uniform clothing, and learned to follow orders. Neatness and personal hygiene were not merely suggested but demanded. Obedience and commitment were mandatory knowing that one day our lives might depend on each of us doing what we had been trained to do and when we were told to do it. All this permanently marked my life.

Lessons learned and habits formed early in life leave an indelible impact. One lesson for me was to understand I needed to learn to follow, before I was equipped to lead my family or others. I needed to know what it was like to take orders, before I issued them to others.

There are times to walk alone. But I decided there are also times when we need to submit to the common discipline of our community. Not as mindless robots, but willingly, and only opting out when human orders violate those of God.

Different circumstances require different roles: Alone. As followers. Or, as leaders. A wise person knows the difference.

From Grandpa With Love

There is a time for everything…
a time for war and a time for peace.
(Ecclesiastes 3:1a, 8b)

A Time For War—And Peace

Age 16-21

11 *"The War is Finally Over! Thank God!"*

After two atomic bombs in early August of 1945, it appeared Japan would surrender. But on August 14, we were informed the war was on again, and ordered to strike the Akita refinery at the north end of the main island. I described our anxiety this way in my diary:

> *Tonite is <u>the</u> nite. We go on the longest bombing range ever conceived by man. Nearly 4000 miles non stop carrying 52 250# bombs and only 6785 gals of gas.*

While still several hundred miles from Guam, the radio operator jumped from his chair and told us the good news. We were ecstatic! Here is my diary entry:

> *Coming home we heard the Big News—after 3/12 years—* **The War is Finally Over! Thank God!**

There is no way to describe our joy and relief. Celebrations went on everywhere. Ours was so big we were grounded for days. It took months to bring the millions of men back to the U.S. I arrived home on July 4, 1946. WWII changed all our lives. At age 20, I summarized it this way in my final diary entry:

> *I wouldn't part with it for a million dollars & I wouldn't go thru it again for another million.*

Few generations escape the awful blight and curse of War. I pray that each one will know how to handle the crises in their lifetime, and we will all realize the only real peace will come from following Jesus and living eternally with Him in His Kingdom!

From Grandpa With Love

Only be careful, and watch yourself closely
so that you do not forget the things your eyes have seen
or let them slip from your heart as long as you live.
Teach them to your children and to their children after them.

(Deuteronomy 4:9)

A Time For War—And Peace

Age 16-21

12 *"I saw you in the nose of the plane."*

It was only about a month after our last bombing mission, and we were landing at an airfield on Hokkaido, a northern Japanese island, to deliver some supplies. I stepped out of the plane and ran into a friend from Wichita. We were both surprised. When he said, *"I saw you in the nose of the plane"*, and I responded, "I wasn't in the nose", we were even more surprised!

Japanese soldiers swarmed all around the plane, bowing, saluting and smiling. We traveled across the dark airfield in an old truck with Japanese all around. I wondered if it was very smart with only a .45 caliber pistol. We had a Japanese interpreter who said he came from the USA to Japan in the early 1930's to receive an estate and they drafted him.

He told us the nearby Academy (which was still operational) was to train men for Kamikaze (suicide) missions. The interpreter told us we could sleep inside the Academy, but we said, "No Thanks!" We all knew the war was over but we didn't feel *that* safe!

Later we talked with Allied prisoners of war who were to be ferried out in my friend's group of C 46 aircraft. I never saw any group of people so happy. They said they had gained 30 pounds per man in four weeks on the supplies the U.S. had flown in. There were English, Dutch, "Aussies" and "Yanks"—from Singapore, Malay, Bataan, Wake Island, etc. We were the first Americans they had seen in three to four years.

There are some memories we never forget—and need to pass on!

From Grandpa With Love

They are spirits of demons performing miraculous signs,

and they go out to the kings of the whole world,

to gather them for the battle

on the great day of God Almighty.

....

Then they gathered the kings together to the place

that in Hebrew is called Armageddon.

(Revelation 16:14, 16)

A Time For War—And Peace

Age 16-21

#13 *"It must be of the spirit if we are to save the flesh."*

In 1945 General Douglas MacArthur, signed the Japanese peace treaty, and broadcast a message which said in part:

"Today the guns are silent. A great tragedy is ended. A great victory has been won. The skies no longer rain death—and the seas bear only commerce—men everywhere walk upright in the sunlight. The entire world is at peace. The holy mission has been completed."

He concluded: *"We have had our last chance. If we do not now devise some greater and more equitable system, Armageddon will be at our door. The problem basically is theological and involves a spiritual recrudescence and improvement of human character that will synchronize with our almost matchless advances in science, art, literature and all material and cultural developments of the past two thousand years. **It must be of the spirit if we are to save the flesh."***

Today, we stand at the same door facing Armageddon. While good economic, political and social institutions are necessary to give us some order and avoid chaos, they will never solve the underlying problem. It still *"must be of the spirit if we are to save the flesh."*

Jesus' answer to General MacArthur's plea was simple: *"But seek first His (God's) Kingdom and His righteousness and all these things will be yours as well."* But I was much older before I finally realized the Kingdom of God starts here on earth. It is *now*!

I intend, therefore, and God willing, to seek, speak, think, live and encourage His Kingdom and His righteousness until I go Home.

From Grandpa With Love

Life as a 24 Hour Day

By Age 21 it is 6:18 a.m.
and
We Choose How to Spend Our "Day"

A Time to Choose—A Wife and Life Work
Age 21-25
(1946-1950)

Listen, my sons, to a father's instructions;

pay attention and gain understanding.

(Proverbs 4:1)

A Time To Choose—A Wife and Life Work

Age 21-25

14 *"All I can tell you, Son, the book is wrong!"*

I attended College and Law School on the G.I. Bill after WWII, which was a new experience for our family. Like many born in the 1800's, my father only graduated from the eighth grade. Also, like many in his generation, he was successful in business and in life.

I was home from Kansas University for a holiday. Dad and I weren't agreeing on some point we were discussing. I finally brought in my textbook. Pointing triumphantly at the page, I said in effect, "See, I am right. It says so right there in my book." Dad didn't bat an eye. He calmly replied, *"All I can tell you, Son, the book is wrong!"*

I was speechless. Although I didn't voice it, I was thinking something very close to, "That stubborn old guy. He won't admit it even when I show him in the book." It was a long time, and many books later that I finally understood how right he had been. And what a great lesson he was teaching me.

I grew up believing if it was in print it was correct. Over the years I have learned how prevalent bad information can be. The problem is worse today as misinformation on social media and the internet is easily passed on to the world as fact.

The lesson has served me well over the years. I strive to write what is true, at least from my perspective. And then often add, "Remember, we all err. So, test what I say, hold onto what is good (of God)—and discard the rest."

From Grandpa With Love

God blessed them and said to them,
"Be fruitful and increase in number; fill the earth and subdue it.
Rule over the fish of the sea and the birds of the air and over every
living creature that moves on the ground."

(Genesis 1:28)

A Time To Choose—A Wife and Life Work

Age 21-25

15 *"I want you to be the father of my children."*

Ellie and I met in the fall of 1946. Thousands of other young men and I had just returned from World War II and enrolled at Kansas University. Girls were in short supply and this was my first date. She was 19 and I was 21. I knew very shortly this was the girl I wanted to marry. I told my folks at Christmas break I wanted her to be my wife.

When I proposed a few weeks later, she didn't just say, "Yes". Instead, she startled me by adding: *"I want you to be the father of my children"*. Her response was remarkably unexpected. It was also prophetic. It told me she was not seeking an outside career. The title of wife and mother was all Ellie ever wanted. Family and friends were her life! We were married August 28, 1948.

For 61 years she was a great gift to me, our children and the generations who followed. At my 90th Birthday celebration, I looked out over the crowd and saw a daughter, two granddaughters and four great granddaughters who carried one of her names! Later, I met separately with the grandchildren and confessed, "If we would have had any idea when we were married that this would be the result, we would have been totally overwhelmed." Then I added, "But it is wonderful!"

Most of us have little idea what it really means to become married. When Ellie answered, *"I want you to be the father of my children"*, she was entrusting me with the greatest honor she could bestow. I didn't realize at the time how much it would enrich us both. I think she did—and I am grateful beyond words.

From Grandpa With Love

For this reason a man will leave his father and mother
and be united to his wife,
and they will become one flesh.

(Genesis 2:24)

A Time To Choose—A Wife and Life Work

Age 21-25

16 *"I do!"*

I vividly remember our wedding day on August 28, 1948. With two of the smallest words in the English language, Ellie and I began the most profound relationship any two people can enjoy in this life. For 61 years we lived and loved, fought and forgave, and had children, grandchildren and now great grandchildren.

At the beginning, I thought married people were to grow together in oneness. At the end, I realized only God could make this happen. At the beginning I thought we could raise children. At the end I knew it was only by the grace of God that children grow up well. At the beginning I thought it was important what I told others. At the end I realized how I lived and modeled were more important.

Like most young people, my only understanding of marriage was watching my parents and other older couples. I had no real understanding of the proper roles of either a husband or wife, until Ellie and I studied and laughed and cried our way through God's instructions. There He graciously showed us His way, including the need to complete, not compete, with one another.

Our marriage was so good it gave me confidence to marry again late in life. That *"I do!"* turned loneliness into a rich P.S. to life.

The world is obviously unraveling. Order is increasingly giving way to chaos. I am convinced that Godly marriage is the bedrock and cornerstone of society. It gives us companionship, children, security and purpose. With it we can prosper and carry on. Without it we will destroy ourselves as a culture and a civilization.

From Grandpa With Love

Blessed is the man who finds wisdom,

the man who gains understanding,

for she is more profitable than silver

and yields better returns than gold.

(Proverbs 3:13-14)

A Time To Choose—A Wife and Life Work

Age 21-25

17 *"You can't memorize all this!"*

Kansas University Law School in 1948 was a shock to me. When I climbed the steps to old Green Hall I entered a completely different world.

Success in undergraduate school had been dominated by learning and remembering facts, Memorization was the key. Law school required that we learn about orderly statutes and other codified laws, and then understand and apply those principles to a combination of cases involving innumerable circumstances. Memorization was not enough!

Undergraduate grades were usually based on class recitations, periodic tests and finals. In Law School we read, discussed and worked all semester—then succeeded or failed in each course based solely on one 4 hour written examination at the end!

Despite my best efforts I could only achieve mediocre grades. The answer finally came one day in the Law Library as I surveyed hundreds of volumes and thought, *"You can't memorize all this!"*

I decided I needed to *think!* I continued to study the statutes and the cases, but I also started *really thinking on my own.* It was exhilarating, but terrifying! Especially, when I minored in memorization, and majored in *thinking* through the answers to the 4 hour tests. But it worked!

That was over 65 years ago, and it changed my life. It is a risk to begin to think for ourselves, but it is the only way to be who God made us to be. I am grateful to Him beyond words.

From Grandpa With Love

41

"For I tell you that unless your righteousness surpasses that of the Pharisees and the teachers of the law, you will certainly not enter the kingdom of heaven."

(Matthew 5:20)

A Time To Choose—A Wife and Life Work

Age 21-25

18 *"Is it ethical?"*

At the outset of our first final exam in Law School, the professor startled us by handing out the test questions and announcing that he was leaving the room while we took the test. He explained, in effect, "You will be in charge of the justice system of the state of Kansas. You must learn now to police yourselves, because it is up to lawyers to keep each other honest. If we can't trust you during examinations, you will never be able to do it later when you are in charge!"

In those earlier years, our code of ethics was summarized on one sheet of paper, posted on a wall in the office. It was best characterized by a story told about an older, respected attorney who was asked to attend a firm meeting about some matter and determine, **"Is it ethical?"** He entered the room and announced, in essence, "If we have to meet to talk about whether it is ethical, then we won't do it." That's ethics!

Although there have been many advancements in the intervening years, e.g. more racial justice, it has been heartbreaking to see the gradual erosion of many moral and ethical standards and principles. As someone has noted, "The unthinkable becomes thinkable; the thinkable becomes doable; and the doable becomes the norm!"

It helped when we had a culture that wanted to do right. Since that is fading, the old lawyer's conclusion is still a good standard for me: "If there is a question, we won't do it."

From Grandpa With Love

Life as a 24 Hour Day

By Age 25 it is 7:30 a.m.
and
We Get Underway and the Action Begins

A Time to Begin—A Family and Law Practice
Age 25-30
(1950-1955)

45

A woman giving birth to a child has pain

because her time has come;

but when her baby is born she forgets the anguish

because of her joy that a child is born into the world.

(John 16:21)

A Time to Begin—A Family and Law Practice

Age 25-30

19 *"It's a girl!"*

Our first child was born in 1950, while I was in Law School. Housing facilities were scarce due to thousands of returning service men. We lived in the upstairs of an old home with linoleum floors and shared a bathroom downstairs with the 90 year old landlord and his wife. Ellie's pregnancy made it difficult for her to use the stairs, so we reverted to a makeshift porta-potty.

The delivery room was in the basement of the old hospital at Lawrence, Kansas. Husbands were not allowed, so my wife's parents and I congregated in the hall waiting for the news. Occasionally the delivery room door would open and I could hear the doctor whistling while he worked! For him, it was another day's work. For me it was trauma!

I suppose everyone has deep memories of the delivery of their first child. Mine is indelibly etched. The doctor charged us $75, just half of the regular $150. Not much now, but a mountain, then. Sensing my anxiety, my father-in-law asked if I wanted to borrow $500. I'm not sure who felt the most relieved when I said, "No!"

When she finally arrived and they announced *"It's a girl!"* I was overwhelmed. I voiced silently, but thankfully, "God has allowed me to be involved in the creation of a life!" Truly a miracle!

In later years He brought us four more miracles. Each one has been a blessing and I am still overwhelmed at His goodness.

Thanks, Lord, for trusting us to be involved with You—and for the beautiful new lives you brought into our lives!

From Grandpa With Love

A man can do nothing better
than to eat and drink and find satisfaction in his work.
This, too, I see, is from the hand of God
(Ecclesiastes 2:24)

A Time to Begin—A Family and Law Practice

Age 25-30

20 *"Are you coming to work here?"*

I graduated from Law School in 1951. Beginning lawyers were not in demand. When one sole practitioner offered me a job, and then called shortly afterward asking, *"Are you coming to work here?"* I quickly agreed.

The office was in a large downtown building, which in those days had spittoons in the hallways and elevator operators. The pay was $250 per month and one-fourth of all the business I could generate. That netted me an additional $150 the first year!

I had no concept at the time how much that phone call, and my response, would impact my entire professional career. Early training by our parents sets the values and disciplines that affect our thoughts and actions throughout all our lives. And initial bosses have great influence on the values and disciplines we will use throughout our work lives. Our first job is *very* important.

Fortunately for me, my employer was an honest man. He modeled ethical behavior and never asked me to do anything improper or questionable. He gave me direction but great freedom to learn. His longtime secretary showed me the practical side and kept me from making too many first-time mistakes.

The older attorney died years ago. But I only recently attended the funeral of his faithful secretary. Sitting there I thought again of how much those two had affected my life.

I shall always be grateful for the phone call, the offer, and the people who started me in the right direction.

From Grandpa With Love

Then the Lord replied:

"Write down the revelation and make it plain on tablets

so that a herald may run with it ......"

(Habakkuk 2:2)

A Time to Begin—A Family and Law Practice

Age 25-30

21 *"Then say it so I can understand it!"*

It was my first jury trial. I was excited, but also nervous and apprehensive. I wanted to do a good job and worked many hours on the Opening Statement. To get my wife Ellie's reaction (and probably her assurance) I read it to her shortly before the trial. I expected her approval and was offended when she asked instead, "Why don't you say 'this' and 'this' and 'this'". Hurt, I countered, "I did just say that!" She didn't miss a beat and promptly fired back, *"Then say it so I can understand it!"*

Ellie's candid but blunt response gave me two challenges:
- To let go of my pride and learn from honest reproof;
- To communicate so clearly and simply that others do comprehend and understand what I am saying.

The first required a change in attitude. It says in the book of Proverbs that wise men love those who reprove them. I decided to try and be wise.

The second required a lifetime of work. My role as a word-worker showed me a lot of lessons. Here are a few:
- Forget myself and get into the listeners' shoes.
- Always speak the truth.
- Use bite-sized language.
- Follow Jesus's example and tell stories with a point.

I was once told "Some people speak in three course dinners and some speak in hash." Ellie, and everyone else who tried to help me be a better cook, have my sincere thanks!

From Grandpa With Love

The first to present his case seems right,
til another comes forward and questions him.

(Proverbs 18:17)

A Time to Begin—A Family and Law Practice

Age 25-30

22 *"We've got the facts!"*

My boss made it clear when I started the practice of law in his one man office in 1951 that I was to handle any litigation. The problem was, I wasn't fully equipped. In those days Law School gave us some theory, a chance to watch lawyers try a case, and participate in one moot course case. Then we were on our own!

I knew I needed more training, so I began to watch and listen to the good, older lawyers when they were trying cases. Lawsuits were tried in the old court house where the only place to eat was a standup bar. Segregation was still the law, but fortunately for me, not at that standup bar. That is where I came to know Ambrose Woodard, a legendary, older African American attorney known throughout the area for his wit, his wisdom and his trial ability.

One case made an indelible impression. I can still see him and hear his slow drawl as he said something like this to the jury: "Mr. (the opposing lawyer) is a smart man. He is really a smart man. He really knows the law. In fact he has the law." But then he added triumphantly, with his wry grin, *"We've got the facts!"*

That one line statement has served me well over my lifetime. No matter how much we know, it doesn't help much if we don't apply the facts. A friend of mine often quotes a Living Bible verse that says in essence, "Above all, get the facts". Today, we are deluged with information from innumerable sources. Many of our so-called "facts" come from unknown people on social media.

I am still grateful for that early lesson to a young lawyer. I still want to be sure, *"We've got the facts!"* Thanks, Ambrose.

From Grandpa With Love

53

Life as a 24 Hour Day

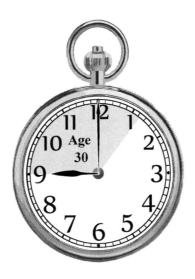

By Age 30 it is 9:00 a.m.
and
We Become Very Busy Working and Playing

A Time to Make a Name—And Seek God
Age 30-44
(1955-1969)

Greater love has no one than this,
that he lay down his life for his friends.
(John 15:13)

A Time to Make a Name—And Seek God

Age 30-44

23 *"Who do you do business with—your enemies?"*

When I decided in 1956, at age 30, to open a new office, I had about $300, a wife, three children and lots of hope! After practicing four years with an older lawyer, I had a sprinkling of new clients, but I knew I needed more to survive.

Since we couldn't advertise or solicit, we needed to find acceptable ways to grow. I gave seminars and did some other unpaid work, but remained troubled how to handle one area. I told my wife Ellie we were raised to believe you never did business with friends or relatives to avoid conflicts that might injure our relationships. With her usual practical sense and candor she asked pointedly, *"Who do you do business with—your enemies?"*

Her frank remark hit home. The result was to welcome close relationships and work with clients as people and not objects in a monopoly game. It took patience but it was worth it. Over the years many of our friends became clients and many of our clients became friends.

The practice of law is often an adversarial process. It may be easier to remain detached and indifferent to the human cost of conflict, but it can also make us hard and calloused. There are exceptions, of course, when we may be too close to be objective and we need to step aside. But, in the main, working with those we knew and getting to know those we worked with, proved to be much better.

Each relationship enriched my life, and I thank them all. And Ellie, too!

From Grandpa With Love

A good name is more desirable than great riches;

to be esteemed is better than silver or gold.

(Proverbs 22:1)

A Time to Make a Name—And Seek God

Age 30-44

24 *"We earn a reputation; we buy advertising."*

It was unethical in the 1950's to advertise for clients. We were a "profession" and were to work only for those who asked us, not demean the profession by asking others for work.

The result was that older established firms did well with their repeat clients and public recognition. But it usually took years of waiting to be asked and patiently building a reputation for young lawyers to become self-sufficient. Although the system was slow, difficult, and sometimes abused, it seemed to produce a sense of worth and responsibility that was healthy for the lawyers and the community.

That all changed when the courts decided the public would be better served if lawyers would compete against one another. The flood gates were opened, and solicitation and massive advertising began. Today, they are commonplace.

There is a maxim, *"We earn a reputation; we buy advertising."* Advertising is like debt: both give us a fast start, but there is a cost for each. Properly used, both can have some benefits. When either is abused, there is a high price personally and as a society.

As an old man, I can't help but wonder if the cost of our private, corporate and government debt, or the cost of competition, advertising and solicitation by lawyers has been worth it.

Most of us believe life has always been like it is in our generation. Old men know that isn't true.

But it takes a long time to get old.

From Grandpa With Love

The glory of young men is their strength,
gray hair the splendor of the old.
(Proverbs 20:29)

A Time to Make a Name—And Seek God

Age 30-44

25 *"But what will we do if we have a problem?"*

It is much easier and more comfortable to reminisce about our early years than it was to live them. As has been said, "War stories are more fun than wars!" But to encourage you in your own recollections, let me share a favorite story one of my early clients enjoyed relating about the beginning of our relationship.

My young friend was taking responsibility for their family business and he wanted to build his own team. I will never forget the day he brought his father to discuss our representation of their company. What must that older gentleman have thought as he entered my small office, with its used desk and two wooden straight back chairs! Here he was talking with a young, relatively inexperienced, lawyer about to be entrusted with legal responsibility for the company he had been building for years.

As expected, my friend indicated he wanted to use our small, two man firm as he went forward with managing their company. His father's reply was a classic, "That's all right, Son", he said. *"But what will we do if we have a problem?"*

It was many years before I fully realized I had learned two very valuable lessons. First, was the encouragement I received from my young friend's willingness to trust me before I was seasoned.

But even more important was the example of his father's courage in taking a risk so that the next generation could move forward.

I am very grateful for both. And, also, that our relationship lasted nearly 40 years, until I retired!

From Grandpa With Love

Do not be anxious about anything,
but in everything, by prayer and petition, with thanksgiving,
present your requests to God.

(Philippians 4:6)

A Time to Make a Name—And Seek God

Age 30-44

26 *"Let's pray!"*

My wife and I, like many young couples after WWII, had been brought up in the Christian faith and attended and married in a denominational church. We didn't know exactly where we were in our faith journey, but we knew it was important to find a church home for our children.

When we moved back to Wichita with our first child, we began our search. Our choice was practical, if not very theological: we chose a large mainline downtown church where our daughter didn't cry in the nursery!

About five years and two children later we moved into a new development where a new small mission church was being started. One day the pastor called on us and invited us to attend. Before leaving, he calmly announced, *"Let's pray!"* We had prayed alone or in church settings, but not at home with a stranger. We were startled, but we found it attractive, and began to attend.

For almost forty years we were fed and nourished as our family, our faith and the congregation all grew. Ellie and I listened, read, studied, taught, served, agreed and disagreed. Our children were fed and nourished in Sunday school, church services, camp settings, retreats and several were married in the sanctuary. We all developed friendships and relationships that still exist today.

The pastor's open prayer life and invitation dramatically changed the course of all our lives.

I wonder where we would be if he hadn't said, *"Let's pray!"*

From Grandpa With Love

Let us discern for ourselves what is right;
let us learn together what is good.

(Job 34:4)

A Time to Make a Name—And Seek God

Age 30-44

27 *"Go learn about labor law!"*

Being young and on our own is an exhilarating experience. The difficulty is we often don't know very much.

A few months after we opened our small two man office, I received an unexpected call from a client. Union pickets had appeared in front of the building being constructed for the company and he was concerned it would delay their opening. When I explained that I was not prepared to handle that kind of situation, his response was typical for many of the entrepreneurs I came to know over the years: *"Go learn about labor law!"*

In those days most labor law work was in the larger cities so I headed (by train) for Kansas City. I visited the National Labor Relations Board office and spent time with a knowledgeable labor lawyer. After two or three days I returned home, and proceeded to practice labor law. That case led to another and then another. Before long it was my principle area of work. And so it continued for almost 40 years.

Years later, another older lawyer and I were reliving some of our early experiences. "Why", we asked ourselves, "would we take any case and get educated when we were young but become so cautious later?" I suppose one reason is that young folks often don't have much to lose. But isn't it really because we are supposed to be bold and take more risk when we are younger? Isn't it the way we are made?

I have concluded we ought to live our age at each time of life. There is a time to be old—but it is when we *are* old!

From Grandpa With Love

But in your hearts set apart Christ as Lord.
Always be prepared to give an answer to everyone who asks you to
give the reason for the hope that you have.   But do this with
gentleness and respect…

(1 Peter 3:15)

A Time to Make a Name—And Seek God

Age 30-44

28 *"This I Believe!"*

During the 1950's a popular series appeared on television in which various people were encouraged to write their personal beliefs and share them on the screen. I was struggling with my own faith and took the challenge to help me find direction for my life.

On July 22, 1959 (a few days before my 34th birthday), alone in my office, I typed out a rather lengthy statement, (that I updated shortly after I reached age 36), entitled, *"This I Believe"*. In essence, I believed I was in control of my destiny. It was as if God put the world together and it was up to us to make it all work out right (which we believed we could do); and it was also up to us to live so we could get into Heaven when we die.

I have often been asked by younger people, "What do you wish you had done differently?" And the answer is always the same: "I wish I had surrendered and started to follow Jesus earlier in life, rather than trying to get to Heaven on my own."

But I have learned we must live each age based on what we hear, see and understand at that time. Some of us find faith as little children. Others during what have been dubbed the "traumatic teens", or the "twinkling twenties". And one man I know said he had Social Security before he received eternal security.

Faith is a gift. Sometimes we are able to *"hear...see... understand ...and turn"* early in life, and sometimes it takes many years, as it did with me.

But I do get cold chills, when I think I could have been too late!

From Grandpa With Love

He who answers before listening—

that is his folly and his shame.

(Proverbs 18:13)

A Time to Make a Name—And Seek God

Age 30-44

29 *"First, let's determine the problem!"*

"What shall we do first?" asked the older company president facing me across his desk.

It was many years ago, and I was a young lawyer beginning to work in the area of labor relations. My client and I were discussing a crisis that I would watch repeated scores of times. Union agents were attempting to organize the plant workers and convince them to go union. The work force was torn, productivity was going down, and what had apparently been a peaceful, normal business a few weeks before had become a hostile battleground.

With all the exuberance of youth, I quickly outlined proposed solutions and courses of action. After patiently listening until I was finished, my older and wiser friend said, "I don't think that's what we should do first. *"First, let's determine the problem!"*

His calm advice served me well over the years. Different problems required different solutions. But first I needed to figure out the problem. Getting the judge or the jury to answer the right question was often the difference between winning and losing. Realizing that issues are often more about relationships than about money began to resolve disputes. Knowing I can't see why others are upset unless I put myself in their shoes, started opening doors for dialogue and peace. And recognizing that God has instructed us to serve, rather than to win, can revolutionize our world.

Jesus has promised us answers if we ask Him. But it sure helps to know the right question!

From Grandpa With Love

Then you will understand
what is right and just and fair—
every good path.

(Proverbs 2:9)

A Time to Make a Name—And Seek God

Age 30-44

30 *"The Rotary Four Way Test"*

One of the most challenging issues for me was how to practice my faith in the marketplace, and not merely be a Sunday/Church believer. The Wichita Rotary Club helped. For almost 40 years I met weekly with other business and professional men (later the club was expanded to include women) to serve and hear speakers who encouraged and inspired us both individually and as a group.

"The Rotary Four Way Test", one of the most widely-known codes of ethics in force today, was the foundational premise. It asked four questions: "Is it the truth?" and then adds, "Is it fair to all concerned? Will it build good will and better friendships? Will it be beneficial to all concerned?"

The test was written by Herbert J. Taylor in 1932 while he was president of a struggling cooking utensil firm in Oklahoma. Taylor's own individual conscience was deeply marked by the Scriptures, and he reportedly memorized and recited each day the Sermon on the Mount. In 1954, while he was President, Taylor made the Four Way Test available to Rotary International. Today, over a million Rotarians worldwide have a higher ethical standard because of his influence.

As the world grows more secular, and becomes more interested in materialism than morality, and more dedicated to winning than to serving, each of us has to decide how we will respond.

I am deeply grateful for Rotary, Herbert J. Taylor, and many Rotarians like him, for modeling and showing a better way.

From Grandpa With Love

You intended to harm me, but God intended it for good
to accomplish what is now being done,
the saving of many lives.
(Genesis 50:20)

A Time to Make a Name—And Seek God

Age 30-44

31 *"Bomb Shatters Interior of Attorneys' Offices"*

As the years progressed, my law practice became largely centered on management's role in employer-employee relations. I was aware of the destruction, violence and intimidation sometimes connected with strikes, but I thought we lawyers were safe.

This all changed one cold night in February, 1964, when the telephone rang about 12:30 a.m., and my law partner announced, "I just received a call from the police department. Our office has been bombed!" When I arrived, the place was a mess: broken windows, ceilings ripped apart, and doors blasted off their hinges. A simple, homemade concussion bomb had done its work!

The next morning the newspapers again carried headlines similar to those which had become familiar to me over the years, but now for the first time, were very real and personal:

"Bomb Shatters Interior of Attorneys' Offices"

I had heard about industrial civil war and viewed its disastrous effects as a lawyer, but now I understood it on a *personal* level!

Knowing *about* something and *personally* experiencing it are entirely different. It often changes our life, sometimes dramatically. After having *our* office bombed, I found myself gradually more interested in building harmony in the workplace, rather than coming in after the fact and trying to win the war.

Looking back it seems whoever threw the bomb meant it for evil, but God used it for good. I have found He often does that—especially if we are relying on Him, not just ourselves.

From Grandpa With Love

73

Settle matters quickly with your adversary who is taking you to court. Do it while you are still with him on the way, or he may hand you over to the judge, and the judge may hand you over to the officer, and you may be thrown into prison. I tell you the truth, you will not get out until you have paid the last penny.

(Matthew 5:25-26)

A Time to Make a Name—And Seek God

Age 30-44

32 *"Watch out for the back side of the sword!"*

It was early in my career. I was sitting in the office of the general counsel of a company I had been asked to represent for some labor problems. We were discussing litigation when he turned to me and exclaimed, *"Watch out for the back side of the sword!"*

It was a new term for me, so I listened attentively. He said they had filed a lawsuit and the defendant immediately filed a counter claim. The final result: the company lost their case and the defendant was awarded substantial damages on the counter claim.

Over the years I thought of this scenario many times. The reality is that it is easy to file a lawsuit, but it can be like the brier-patch Peter Rabbit found was very hard to get out of, once he got involved.

God has given us the institution of worldly government to keep peace with outsiders and to judge disputes for those under its control. But simply because we have a forum and the right to file lawsuits doesn't mean it is always wise. The Bible issues warnings about such controversies and encourages us to resolve disputes before they enter the courtroom.

As a younger lawyer, I often found myself fighting labor wars. Strikes, litigation, and even violence were common. But it took its toll on me, personally, as well as on my clients.

I decided litigation is to the law what surgery is to the body. Both are sometimes necessary, but they don't give anesthetics for lawsuits!

From Grandpa With Love

My dear brothers, take note of this: everyone should be quick to listen, slow to speak and slow to become angry

(James 1:19)

A Time to Make a Name—And Seek God

Age 30-44

33 *"She asked three times—and no one heard her!"*

Supper-time with two adults and six, (including our nephew) growing youngsters around one large table was interesting. (Some might use another word!) But it was one of the most joyous times of our family life. And a time we often learned from one another.

I sat at one end and their mother Ellie at the other. One evening our youngest daughter who was about three at the time, was seated at my right hand. After we said the blessing the food began to flow and the conversation began to grow. Gradually, the din grew louder and louder, which was familiar, but still noisy.

Suddenly I realized our three year old was calmly crawling out of her chair, walking across the table and picking up the butter dish! I, of course, started to come unglued! But one of the older boys stopped me when he came to her defense: *"She asked three times—and no one heard her!"*

I learned we all want to be heard. We want someone to listen, whether we are three or thirty or ninety years old. We need someone to hear us and listen to us even if we are the least significant in the eyes of the world.

The lesson was reinforced years later when I unconsciously opened a friend's car door in anticipation of getting out when he was finished. He stopped in midsentence and announced abruptly, "Goodbye!" "You weren't through", I protested. He answered simply, "You were!"!

It takes a little effort, but it does pay to listen when others speak!

From Grandpa With Love

The more the words, the less the meaning,
and how does that profit anyone?

(Ecclesiastes 6:11)

A Time to Make a Name—And Seek God

Age 30-44

34 *"Simplify! Simplify! Simplify!"*

Three thousand years ago, the writer of the Book of Ecclesiastes (who was probably King Solomon) posed a most interesting rhetorical question: *"The more the words, the less the meaning, and how does that profit anyone?"* (Ecclesiastes 6:11 NIV)

After years of word working, I am convinced the power of words is often inversely proportional to their number.

It has been said, "If you want me to speak an hour, I am ready now. If you want me to speak for two minutes, it will take me two weeks to prepare."

The *"Lord's Prayer"* can be recited in about 30 seconds; the *"Ten Commandments"* in about 2 minutes; and the *"Sermon on the Mount"* in about 20 minutes. Innumerable books and articles have been written about each of these, yet the original power-packed documents are very short. The same holds true in more modern times, as we are awed by the brevity of the *"Declaration of Independence"* and Lincoln's *"Gettysburg Address"*, both of which have become models for those who would learn how to speak and write briefly and effectively.

When the Apostle, Paul, was on trial for his life, he set forth his defense as recorded in the 26th chapter of the Book of Acts in the Bible. His plea can be read in about 5 minutes. Yet the Judge was so convicted by his words, that the *Judge* got up and left the room!

I guess, *"Simplify! Simplify! Simplify!"* is still good advice!

From Grandpa With Love

79

The length of our days is seventy years—or eighty,

if we have the strength; yet their span is but trouble and sorrow,

for they quickly pass, and we fly away.

......

Teach us to number our days aright,

that we may gain a heart of wisdom.

(Psalm 90:10, 12)

A Time to Make a Name—And Seek God

Age 30-44

35 *"Middle Age: A Normal Crisis"*

One of the most impactful speeches I ever heard was entitled, ***"Middle Age: A Normal Crisis"***. The Rotary speaker was a psychiatrist in a world renowned clinic, who said he chose the subject because it was where he was in life. So was I—and I was ripe for his comments which I still recall fifty years later!

The heart of the message was this: The normal life span is about 80 years. Since we can see ahead about as far as behind, we often realize around age forty, we are going to die. We may feel frustrated, bewildered and sometimes broken by having lost a job, a promotion, or a marriage. We believe we are rapidly becoming what we're going to be and it's not what we wanted or hoped, and we are searching for answers. Thus the term, "the funky forties"!

Some buy sports cars and/or remarry to try and have it all before it's too late. Others change careers, similar to about half of the seminary students I met on a trip to Israel who were making a mid-life correction to go from the work world to the church world.

The key is to recognize it is change time and deal with it!

I didn't realize it at the time, but the next few years were going to usher in the most significant life changes I would ever experience. They would affect my family, my career, and most of all, my eternal destiny. I cannot imagine where I and others in my world might be today if God had not graciously guided me.

The speaker—and the Lord—have my gratitude and thanks!

From Grandpa With Love

Sitting down, Jesus called the Twelve and said,
"If anyone wants to be first,
he must be the very last, and the servant of all."
(Mark 9:35)

A Time to Make a Name—And Seek God

Age 30-44

#36 *"Somebody has to be second!"*

Since we couldn't advertise when I began practicing law in 1951, it was a challenge to get business. When a client asked me to learn about labor law, it was a relatively new area and I began to make a name for myself. As the years passed, I decided being *the best* in something paid off, and it became a part of my belief system.

Later, I spoke of this to our children and one of our sons responded rather incredulously, "But Dad! *Somebody has to be second!"* Frankly, I had come to the place where that thought had not occurred to me. I knew being *the best* in one area of law was working for me, and I was unconsciously (and perhaps even consciously) giving it as an unwritten law for our family.

Much later one of our children startled me with a comment that made even clearer the unfair yoke I had placed on them: "You gave us a family bent that shamed us. You told us we had to be the best of something, and if we weren't we felt ashamed!"

What a mistake! Being successful isn't a matter of comparison. That only builds pride if we do well and shame if we do not. The answer is simply to be the best we can be. It has nothing to do with how we compare with others.

The real test of success is not to be *the best* of anything—but rather, to be whatever God designed us to be. That may be first and it may be last. In fact, in His Kingdom, He tells us the best place is to be last, so we can serve others!

I am glad our family learned the truth before it was too late.

From Grandpa With Love

Going a little farther,

he fell with his face to the ground and prayed,

"My Father, if it is possible, may this cup be taken from me.

Yet not as I will, as you will."

(Matthew 26:39)

A Time to Make a Name—And Seek God

Age 30-44

#37 *"The secret of the will"*

The 1960's were traumatic. Assassinations, the Viet Nam war, riots and campus chaos rocked the nation. Ellie and I were in the "funky forties" and many of our children in the "traumatic teens." And I was silently struggling with the eternal question all of us must ultimately face: "What is the real purpose of life?"

I discovered there were two answers: mine and God's. My answer was to live to satisfy my own desire for pleasure, position, power and possessions. The quest for these temporary goals also became the anesthetic I used to shield myself from facing the question of eternity and how I would spend it. By contrast, God wanted me to surrender to Him and let Him lead me to those things that would provide not only present fulfillment, but also eternal purpose and meaning to my life and the activities in which I was engaged.

But I was afraid to surrender and trust God. As a friend later challenged me, "You reminded me of a drunk sitting in the gutter who wouldn't give control of his life to God, because he was afraid He would make a mess of it!"

Fortunately, the book, *Beyond Ourselves,* by Catherine Marshall introduced me to *"The secret of the will".* I finally realized it isn't an issue of desire or emotion, but of the will. Jesus left us the model as He faced the cross and prayed, *"Yet not as I will, but as you will";* and again in the Lord's Prayer, *"...your kingdom come, your will be done on earth as it is in heaven."*

The real issue is this: Is God's will or mine going to rule?

From Grandpa With Love

For it is by grace you have been saved, through faith—
and this is not from yourselves—it is the gift of God,
not by works, so that no one can boast.

(Ephesians 2:8-9)

A Time to Make a Name—And Seek God

Age 30-44

38 *"Lord, I commit all of myself to you that I am able; and I accept Jesus as your divine Son."*

As we approached the last of the 1960's, I sensed that my spiritual journey was about to reach a turning point. The struggle had been growing with increasing intensity over the preceding years. I had read the Bible, taught and even spoken from the pulpit, but I knew the person I was trying to build was not adequate, nor complete.

Finally, in true labor lawyer style, I negotiated a settlement with God. I couldn't bring myself to surrender my will in one step, but I agreed in the early summer of 1969 I would surrender on August 10, 1969, my 44th birthday

My birthday finally arrived. Following a celebration with my family, and without advising anyone of my intentions, I walked up the stairway, down the hallway, into our bedroom. There I knelt alone and confessed something like this:

"Lord, I commit all of myself to you that I am able; and I accept Jesus as your divine Son."

Without realizing it, I was born again spiritually on the anniversary of the day I was born physically. My physical and spiritual birthdays were the same—but 44 years apart! For me there were no flashing lights or emotional outbursts at the time. But that birthday did mark the death of my old life and the beginning of a new life in Christ and His Kingdom.

Faith is a gift. But I finally realized we must humble ourselves, surrender our will, and receive the gift in order to have it!

From Grandpa With Love

Part II

Going God's Way

Age 44-On

Life as a 24 Hour Day

By Age 44 it is 1:12 p.m.
and
We See it is "Mid-Day" and Change Course

A Time to Receive—and Use God's Gifts
Age 44-60
(1969-1985)

For everyone who asks receives;
he who seeks finds;
and to him who knocks, the door will be opened.

(Matthew 7:8)

A Time to Receive—and Use God's Gifts

Age 44-60

39 *"You need to go to Bear Trap Ranch!"*

After I surrendered at age 44, in 1969, and agreed to follow Jesus, I was unsure what to do next. I turned to our pastor for direction. After a few sessions, he said, *"You need to go to Bear Trap Ranch!"* So Ellie and I, with some of children, arranged to attend a week-long session at the Intervarsity Conference Center near Colorado Springs.

After a day or two, the President, who was also a layman, sensing how green and new I was, asked me pointedly, "How did you get here, anyway?" I think it was obvious to both of us it was of God. For the next several days we heard speakers, interacted with other searchers and grew in the Lord.

This experience was the beginning of a lifelong participation in a para-church world I never knew existed. Like many others of my generation, I had a narrow understanding of "church". Now I began to see it as the whole body of Christ. And the form often changes to meet the needs of various times, places and cultures.

Meeting in conferences, small groups, and one-on-one; evangelizing, teaching and nurturing; organizations such as Intervarsity, World Impact, Basic Youth Conflicts, Navigators, Yokefellows, The fellowship, Laity Lodge, Christian Legal Society, and on and on, augment the work of local churches. And participating with them has fed me and helped fill my ravenous hunger for God's word and real fellowship for the last forty years.

How grateful I am to the Lord, my Pastor, and Bear Trap Ranch and its faithful people for opening the door to this new world!

From Grandpa With Love

93

We proclaim to you what we have seen and heard,

so that you may have fellowship with us.

And our fellowship is with the Father

and with His Son, Jesus Christ.

(1John 1:3)

A Time to Receive—and Use God's Gifts

Age 44-60

40 *"I've been reading about Christian fellowship— and I'd like to know where I can get some."*

After starting to follow Jesus, I was hungry for more. I read about Christian fellowship but I wasn't experiencing it. I took a chance and called a new-in-town businessman who seemed open about his faith. My request was simple: *"I've been reading about Christian fellowship—and I'd like to know where I can get some."*

He didn't give me a list of books or the name of a pastor. Rather, he began to spend time with me himself. For three years we met together and with others, praying, studying, learning, memorizing scripture, traveling, and sharing our faith. He didn't teach me *about* Christian fellowship. *He helped me experience it!*

There are many things in life that cannot be understood intellectually; they must be experienced. One little boy, when asked what his grape sucker tasted like, thought a moment and then said, "Here, have a bite!" No words can convey the fragrance of a flower or the exhilaration of new love. They must be experienced.

And so it is with Christian fellowship. I had known the fellowship of working with others, serving with others in the military or an organization, or playing with others in a sport or game. These are good but not the best. The best comes when we become one with Christ and with other believers. When we come together in Christ, to pray or work or share, we experience *Christian* fellowship!

But it didn't happen until I humbled myself and asked!

From Grandpa With Love

95

A word aptly spoken is like apples of gold

in settings of silver.

(Proverbs 25:11)

A Time to Receive—and Use God's Gifts

Age 44-60

#41 ***"You sure have pretty shoes!"***

Our youngest daughter arrived when Ellie was in her late thirties and I had just turned forty. It was somewhat different, so I and two other men in like circumstances, informally named ourselves "The Over-Forty Fathers Club." But it was a wonderful blessing!

However, as our little girl grew, it became a bit of a social problem. What was perfectly normal to our family seemed unusual to some of our daughter's little friends. Being normal young girls, they were curious. And when young girls are curious they look, and think, and finally ask questions.

During an afternoon dancing class, our seven or eight year old daughter ambled over and quietly told her mother, "That girl over there wants to know if you are my mother or my grandmother." Armed with the answer, she delivered the response. A short time later she returned and announced, "She wants to know how old you are." And, after looking up a moment, she queried thoughtfully, "Are you 46 or 64?" Once more she delivered the reply.

When the class session ended and the girls were preparing to disband, our daughter's little friend came over and shyly stood close by my wife. After a moment, and with her eyes still fixed on the floor, she said softly, ***"You sure have pretty shoes!"***

I guess she knew when all else fails, and you want to make up with a lady—compliment her clothes!

From Grandpa With Love

97

He has made everything beautiful in its time.

He has also put eternity in the hearts of men;

yet they cannot fathom what God has done from beginning to end.

(Ecclesiastes 3:11)

A Time to Receive—and Use God's Gifts

Age 44-60

42 *"We have time! Isn't that wonderful? We have time!"*

I was looking for new direction in my late forties. Since I knew no older spiritual grandfather figure locally, I called Dr. Elton Trueblood (probably in his seventies at the time), a widely known writer, speaker, pastor and professor at a small Christian college.

Although I was totally unknown to him, he welcomed my call and invited me to come for a visit. I'll never forget his opening comment which was so unusual in our hurried, harried world: *"We have time! Isn't that wonderful? We have time!"*

He gave me his undivided attention that day, and several other times over the years. He was the first to encourage me to write and offered to critique my work which began my effort to relate the teachings of Jesus and the Bible to everyday life. He helped me comprehend the power and lasting effect of writing, saying, "You can walk with the 'greats'. All you have to do is to take them off the shelves."

One of the most unforgettable challenges he issued to me was his answer when I spoke of our pastor and called him *the* minister. He pointed his finger at me and said emphatically, "Don't ever say *the* minister—every believer is a minister!"

This wise older man's openness, wisdom and gracious pouring out of himself into a younger seeker gave me a model I had never known. It also gave me confidence to seek out other, wise older men who had time and wisdom they were willing to share.

And it made me want to be that same kind of older man!

From Grandpa With Love

When this is done, I will go to the king,

even though it is against the law.

And if I perish, I perish.

(Esther 4:16b)

A Time to Receive—and Use God's Gifts

Age 44-60

43 *"And if I perish, I perish."*

I was concerned clients wanted a tough, no-holds-barred attorney and I would lose business if people found out I was following Jesus. Finally, my wife and I went to Colorado for a week so I could think through the problem.

One afternoon on a hillside near Gunnison, God gave me the answer. It came from the biblical story of Esther as she struggled with whether to reveal her Jewish identity to her pagan husband, the king, and ask him to save her people from being slaughtered. When I read her courageous example, I decided it was time for me to take a stand. So I dedicated my law practice to God and said, like Esther, *"And if I perish, I perish."*

The opportunity soon came to put my declaration to the test. I was listening to a speaker and heard him ask, "Who would be the hardest three people for you to witness to?" I knew immediately, and they were all important clients. With much fear and trembling, and being careful not to impose on work time, I found opportunities to give each of these three men a short summary of my spiritual journey.

In retrospect, I don't know how much my speaking out helped any of these men. I decided I didn't need to know because that is between them and God. But I do know it surely helped me.

It made speaking out easier after this difficult beginning. It drew clients in tune with the work God had given me to do.

And I never perished as a result!

From Grandpa With Love

Now get up and stand on your feet.
I have appeared to you to appoint you as a servant
and as a witness of what you have seen of me
and what I will show you.

(Acts 26:16)

A Time to Receive—and Use God's Gifts

Age 44-60

44 *"Before you go, speak to the congregation."*

After surrendering my will and beginning to follow Jesus, I found myself restless and wanting to make changes. One day, our pastor asked if I would tell the congregation about my new-found faith. When I confessed to him we were thinking of going to another church, he said, "I know", and then added, *"Before you go, speak to the congregation."*

I was reluctant to speak. The sixties had been traumatic with assassinations of the president, his brother and Martin Luther King, the Viet Nam war, civil unrest and the bombing of our law office. Our family was going through the teen years and some difficult medical issues, and my wife had lost her only brother, mother, father and grandmother during the same period. I needed help from others and didn't feel qualified to tell anyone, anything!

But I agreed. At the end of my remarks I invited any who wanted to get together and talk to give me their names. I had no idea what I had set in motion.

About a dozen of us began meeting in our home for a study based on Ray Stedman's book, *Body Life*. We grew to thirty or forty, and loved and learned together for several years. In addition, I received a call shortly after the church service from a man who later came to my office and surrendered his life to Jesus. And I stayed with that congregation for the next 25 years!

I learned much of the journey with Jesus is simply to walk through the doors when He opens them. We don't have to feel good or qualified. Simply listen, and then do what He tells us!

From Grandpa With Love

I in them and you in me.

May they brought to complete unity

to let the world know that you sent me

and have loved them even as you have loved me.

(John 17:23)

A Time to Receive—and Use God's Gifts

Age 44-60

45 *"Can I have your money?"*

It was my 49th birthday and I was looking forward to moving into what someone had described to me as "The Fabulous Fifties". Our whole family was seated around the table just after completing our dinner, and I was feeling philosophical.

"Some time ago," I said, "I heard of a man who was discussing the stages of life. He said when he was a young boy, his greatest desire was for 'food'. As he grew older, his desire changed to 'money', because that would allow him to buy all the food or other things he wanted. Still later, his desire was for 'time', because he found with time he could make the money to buy the things he wanted. But finally, he concluded the most important thing in life was 'relationships'. That is where I am now," I announced as I surveyed all those nearest and dearest to me. "To me, relationships—you all—are the most important thing in life!"

There was quiet for a moment. Then my 19 year old son, with a smile in his eyes, spoke up and said, *"Can I have your money?"*

Earlier in my life, relationships had not been so important to me. As a result, I had found myself living in conflict much of the time. Now, I was beginning to experience one of the greatest rewards of my new life in Christ. And it was not only a blessing for me. It helped everyone around me: family, business and friends.

Relationships truly are the prize of life, but sometimes we don't realize it until we are older and look back.

I often wonder where we would all be if God had not rescued us!

From Grandpa With Love

105

Now when he saw the crowds,
he went up on the mountainside and sat down.
His disciples came to him
and he began to teach them, saying....
(Matthew 5:1-2)

A Time to Receive—and Use God's Gifts

Age 44-60

#46 *"The Sermon on the Mount"*

After committing my life to Jesus, I couldn't seem to get enough of the Bible. I was especially attracted to Mathew 5-7, commonly referred to *"The Sermon on the Mount"*. Like any modern-day sermon it can be read in about 20 minutes, but it is so profound it has inspired almost innumerable books, articles and sermons.

My faith and understanding were immeasurably strengthened as I read, memorized and meditated on these scriptures. Over the years it caused me to write a booklet, then lyrics for a concert, which in turn became a series of poems and short explanation of the Sermon. Each one increased my awe at these God-given words.

Life spelled out in this Sermon is often opposite from life in the world. For example, if we want to be great then be the servant of all. If we want to live forever then we die to ourselves here. If we want to be rich in Heaven then we give up the pursuit of pleasure, possessions, power and position here on earth.

At first I thought following Jesus would make me appear upside down to the rest of the world. But as I read and studied, I finally realized it was the *world* that was upside down!

The Sermon on the Mount has been described as the language of the Kingdom of God. And, like the runner in the movie *Chariots of Fire*, when I speak and live His language, I feel His pleasure.

I can't recite the Sermon from memory any more, but those few words dramatically changed my life—here in this world and for eternity!

From Grandpa With Love

Do not get drunk on wine, which leads to debauchery.

Instead, be filled with the Spirit.

(Ephesians 5:18)

A Time to Receive—and Use God's Gifts

Age 44-60

47 *"I want to be filled with the Holy Spirit!"*

After I surrendered my will and began to follow Jesus, I read a number of accounts about the Holy Spirit experiences of people who had been greatly used by God. I found that Oswald Chambers' tombstone referred to Luke 11:3: *"If you then, though you are evil, know how to give good gifts to your children, how much more will your Father in heaven give the Holy Spirit to those who **ask** Him!"* (Luke 11:13) (Emphasis added)

I began to talk with God and asked in essence, if there is more, if the Holy Spirit is to be involved in my life, I want to have it. *"I want to be filled with the Holy Spirit!"* I heard it was often a very emotional encounter as well as a turning point in life.

My own experience was much the same. I was driving alone on the Kansas Turnpike going to a labor relations session. I had been praying when suddenly and without warning, I was overpowered with emotion. I pulled off the highway and wept and poured myself out to God. I cannot explain it. I do not know if it is to happen to everyone, but I do know it changed me forever.

It was the beginning of a deeper life as I began to know Holy Spirit as a Person. He has guided and encouraged me for the past forty years. Sometimes it has been a word, an incident or simply a sense of peace that I am moving in His will. I wish I could be more definite, but it wasn't clear until it happened.

And it didn't happen until I asked!

From Grandpa With Love

We have different gifts, according to the grace given us.....
if it is showing mercy, let him do it cheerfully.
(Romans 12:6-8)

A Time to Receive—and Use God's Gifts

Age 44-60

48 *"I think you have the gift of mercy."*

The Holy Spirit was much in evidence during the widespread outbreak of faith in the late 1960's and early 1970's. When a friend took us to Dallas to hear Bill Gothard, it was life-changing. Disjointed pieces of the puzzle finally began to fall into place.

Later, we attended a Gothard conference in Los Angeles devoted to understanding and identifying the gifts of the Holy Spirit. When someone said, *"I think you have the gift of mercy"*, I rebelled, afraid it might destroy my career. I related the gift to a nurse in a white hat at the hospital and thought no-one would want a lawyer involved in labor relations, to have such a sensitive gift.

Yet, as I finally accepted God's gracious gift, I found it was a perfect fit, *if* I was not trying to win at all costs but rather to eliminate discord and bring a spirit of reconciliation and harmony into the workplace! When Ellie and I understood each other's gifts it helped resolve our differences and bring us even closer together. And seeing and understanding the spiritual gifts of other believers let us better appreciate and interact with them.

I gradually discovered the Body of Christ contains many gifts and each has a valuable part to play. When we listen to the Holy Spirit speaking through our own gifts and also through the gifts of others around us, we can stop playing a solo, or someone else's instrument, and begin to be a part of the great orchestra of God.

And when we do it in love—real harmony begins!

From Grandpa With Love

For who makes you different from anyone else?
What do you have that you did not receive?
And if you did receive it, why do you boast as though you did not?

((1 Corinthians 4:7)

A Time to Receive—and Use God's Gifts

Age 44-60

49 *"To Marvin, from Marvin, In Love"*

I was taught from an early age to be self-reliant. It was a part of our Depression era upbringing. It took me many years, and one memorable lesson, to learn the gift of receiving. It came through a good friend who told me what I needed to hear, even when I didn't want to receive it.

We were at a Christian bookstore, when I saw a particular book which appealed to me and I mentioned it to my friend. He said, "Let me buy it for you." I declined and indicated I would get it myself. He responded, "Oh, come on, let me buy you the book!"

Instead of graciously accepting his offer, I insisted I would buy the book. He smiled and waited until I returned from paying. Then he said, "Here, let me write in it." I handed it to him, but thought how strange that he wanted to write in the flyleaf when I had bought the book.

When he handed it back to me, I opened the book and read the following statement:

"To Marvin, From Marvin, In Love"

followed by my friend's signature. Now would you like to know the name of the book I had bought for myself? It was,

"Let God Love You!"

It was an embarrassing lesson, but a valuable one. I finally understood that God often shows His love to us through other people—but we have to humble ourselves and receive!

From Grandpa With Love

Then he said to me, "Son of man,
eat this scroll I am giving you and fill your stomach with it."
So I ate it, and it tasted as sweet as honey in my mouth.

(Ezekiel 3:3)

A Time to Receive—and Use God's Gifts

Age 44-60

50 *"What I fed the most grew the most!"*

I guess we always remember our solo flights, the first time we do something new. It happened for me on my first lay witness team attending a "Reach Out" led by evangelist Leighton Ford. On the way down to Oklahoma, my friend witnessed to the filling station owner when we stopped for gas. That was a new one to me.

When we arrived they had us speak at a men's service luncheon. I was to give a short opener, but was so excited I took up the whole presentation time. Then on to a foundry where we spoke with a crew of hot tired men who listened attentively as a jury to decide if they believed that Jesus was who He said He was.

Later we went to a large auditorium meeting where one of the team accepted the challenge to give a 30 second testimony by calmly reciting, "To be above with the saints we love, Oh! that will be glory! But to be below with the saints we know, that's another story!" which was greeted with cheers from the audience.

But it was a much older (and much too fast) driver who was taking us to one of our events who gave me much to ponder when he was asked, "What is the most important thing you have learned in life?" Without slowing a bit, he answered, *"What I fed the most grew the most!"* An answer I have thought on and used many times as the years have passed.

In looking back I decided these trips were primarily to feed us— since God could have used anyone. But thankfully He chose us.

I do hope the ones who heard us got something out of it!

From Grandpa With Love

Fathers, do not exasperate your children;
instead, bring them up in the training and instruction of the Lord.

(Ephesians 6:4)

A Time to Receive—and Use God's Gifts

Age 44-60

51 *"You can put me in my room,*
but you can't make me study!"

I never wrote anything about raising children. It always seemed so easy in the books and so hard in real life. It didn't begin to work for me until I let go and let God be in charge. Then, it was almost as if I was sitting on the fence watching as He directed me.

Each of the children was different. It made me wonder how five kids, raised in the same household by the same parents could have such different abilities, personalities, gifts and needs? One thing that helped was to accept that fact and treat them as individuals and not as a group. Another was to recognize I wasn't their alter ego, and I wasn't supposed to conform them to some great, predetermined plan. I was just supposed to help them become who God had designed them to be.

Over the years they taught me many lessons. One came about half way through a daughter's school career, when in desperation I confined her to her room to study. Her response was a classic: *"You can put me in my room, but you can't make me study!"*

She was teaching me the age-old lesson that you can conform people from the outside by laws, and rules, and force. But we do something *internally* because *we want* to.

There are times, of course, when we have to control children or others for their own benefit. But it sure helped when I learned to make myself, and the way I was going, attractive enough that they followed because they wanted to—not because they had to!

From Grandpa With Love

117

And the things you have heard me say
in the presence of many witnesses
entrust to reliable men who will also be qualified to teach others.

(2 Timothy 2:2)

A Time to Receive—and Use God's Gifts

Age 44-60

52 *"I think it is time for you to start investing your life in other people."*

As I moved into my fifties, I was challenged by a man who had been investing his life in me. He said rather pointedly, *"I think it is time for you to start investing your life in other people."* My answer was honest, but not very spiritual. I responded, "I don't think much of the idea. But because you have asked me, I will!"

I understood pouring into my physical family, but the thought of investing spiritually in others was new to me. But I felt deeply indebted to this former stranger who had taken me under his wing and poured his life into mine, meeting together, praying, memorizing scripture and taking me with him to conferences and opportunities to learn and share our faith with others. I knew I needed to pass it on.

It was one of the major decisions of my life. My world of achievement, accumulation and making a name for myself paled in comparison to the deep satisfaction God gave me as I began to carry out this new role.

One of the best parts has been the knowledge that everything He uses me to invest in other people is eternal. Those investments can't be wiped out. They don't depend on a government guarantee. They won't be affected by stock market crashes, real estate bubbles, or global conflicts.

Jesus told us to lay up lasting treasure in Heaven. For me that will be Him and the people He brought into my life. What a reunion!

From Grandpa With Love

Whoever welcomes one of these little children in my name welcomes me; and whoever welcomes me does not welcome me but the one who sent me.

(Mark 9:37)

A Time to Receive—and Use God's Gifts

Age 44-60

53 *"Always keep your rare-bird net ready!"*

Some people have a rare ability to say things in a way we remember. One of the men who took me with him as he followed Jesus had that gift. And one of the phrases he used became a part of my life.

It happened after he suggested I begin to work with other men. I didn't know where to begin. But it finally fell into place and gave me an unforgettable lesson when he admonished, *"Always keep your rare-bird net ready!"*

That was many years ago and his advice has repeatedly blessed me with men God brought into my life. The easiest were those who, like me, openly called and asked for help. Others didn't voice it, but they were obviously hungry. They didn't know how to ask and seemed relieved and eager when they were invited.

I finally realized all of us have times in life when we are especially teachable. At change times and crisis times, people are often ready to learn, and will reach out for help. At other times they are too busy, it seems, to ask or even to listen. Later these individuals may surface and let us know they are listening and want more.

But however we detect an interest and hunger, it is good to remember my old friend's advice: *"Always keep your rare-bird net ready!"* Then we can extend to them the same "right hand of fellowship" that was offered to me many years ago.

When that happens, we each profit as we walk together with the Lord and one another—and learn from both!

From Grandpa With Love

121

Finally, all of you, live in harmony with one another;

be sympathetic, love as brothers,

be compassionate and humble.

(1 Peter 3:8)

A Time to Receive—and Use God's Gifts

Age 44-60

54 *"Harmony in the Workplace"*

My law practice ultimately centered on labor relations particularly those involving unions. For years, I watched the battles, including bitter, even violent, "strikes" which often left deep scars.

In an effort to find a better way, I analyzed 25 or 30 union disputes we had handled. Each night after work, I would sit in our basement reviewing these cases. I thought the issue would be about money, but I found it was really about relationships, and we usually fought about the money after relationships were broken.

I found four common problems and antidotes: Faulty Supervision needed Servant Leadership; Change needed Communication; Incompetence needed Discipline (as in Disciple) and Divided Houses needed Security. As these principles were taught and applied we began to see relationships strengthened and discord minimized. We named it *"Harmony in the Workplace"*, which ultimately found its way into the *From Grandpa With Love* series.

One of our most precious gifts is relationships—in a business or a family or a church. But we need to be willing to let God use us to be loved and to love in order for relationships to flourish.

It is as if God wants to conduct a wondrous human orchestra, designed to make beautiful music as He fits each unique note in with all the other notes in a *"Heavenly Harmony"* for our enjoyment and His Glory.

I believe the result might be like—or at least close to—being serenaded by the music of a choir of angels!

From Grandpa With Love

123

Humble yourselves, therefore,
under God's mighty hand,
that he may lift you up in due time.

(1 Peter 5:6)

A Time to Receive—and Use God's Gifts

Age 44-60

55 *"Humble yourself under the mighty hand of God!"*

Several of us were invited by a friend to go to Billings, Montana, to share our faith. One night I was asked if I would share my spiritual journey at a breakfast meeting the next morning. Before going to bed my roommate and I knelt and prayed. Like John the Baptist, I asked to become less and that Jesus would be greater.

Little did I know what I was praying!

The next morning we arrived in the large banquet room in the hotel. We saw the stage had been raised several feet above the floor, and there were rough wooden steps leading up to the speakers' platform. As I started up the stairs, one foot slipped, I fell spread-eagled across the stage, and an embarrassed hush descended on the room. I picked myself up and moved to the microphone, and blurted out a jumbled version of St. Peter's statement, *"Humble yourself under the mighty hand of God!"*

Laughter broke the tension, God was glorified and I survived.

The early Apostles were described in the Bible, as *"fools for Christ"*. Sometimes, we do the most to advance God's Kingdom, when we appear the most foolish in the eyes of the world.

God meant for us to act as rivers carrying out into the world what He entrusts to us, although it may be embarrassing, or even dangerous. If I keep His gifts to myself, I can become a Dead Sea: stagnant, stale and smelly.

It has been better simply going ahead and being a "fool"!

From Grandpa With Love

125

However, there should be no poor among you, for in the land the Lord your God is giving to you o possess as your inheritance, he will richly bless you, if only you fully obey the Lord your God and are careful to follow all these commands I am giving you today.

For the Lord your God will bless you as he has promised, and you will lend to many nations but will borrow from none. You will rule over many nations, but none will rule over you.

(Deuteronomy 15:4-6)

A Time to Receive—and Use God's Gifts

Age 44-60

56 *"Live with a margin!"*

Some people like to live on the edge of life. They delight in pushing the boundaries. Thrills and excitement seem to be intoxicating and irresistible. But it wasn't me.

I don't know when it was I realized I was a lot happier when I could *"Live with a margin!"* It became one of the maxims of my life. It removed much of the worry and stress as I learned to "keep a little gas in the tank and a little money in the bank." Starting early for an appointment and retaining a little energy for emergencies was easy and natural for me. It helped me care for myself and those for whom I was responsible.

Today, the world encourages us to "borrow and buy". Instead of accumulating the necessary money to make a purchase, we are increasingly told we should borrow now and pay later. The result has been a massive explosion of debt, personally, in business and in government. That, in turn, has diminished the value of money world-wide, reduced interest on savings to almost zero, and made it seem outdated to save and *"Live with a margin!"*

The ancient Israelites were told if they would follow God's instructions they would borrow from none and lend to many. Our society has not followed that mandate so we are awash in debt and the servant of our lenders.

I realize God expects us to be interdependent, and there are times we need to be willing to accept aid from others. But I have found a margin sure helps *me* do what He has given *me* to do!

From Grandpa With Love

As they were walking along and talking together,

suddenly a chariot of fire and horses of fire appeared

and separated the two of them,

and Elijah went up to heaven in a whirlwind.

(2 Kings 2:11)

A Time to Receive—and Use God's Gifts

Age 44-60

57 *"This time I don't even have to pack my bags!"*

My father died on December 17, 1951 after a severe stroke. I was 26 years old and struggling with my faith. I was upset and literally shaking when I saw him lying still and dead on the hospital bed.

I made a full commitment to follow Jesus in 1969, and my mother died 10 years later Dec 26, 1979. A few days before Christmas she called and said she needed to go to the hospital. When I arrived she was standing on the curb with her bag waiting for me.

Mom spent Christmas in the hospital. Our family was going to Colorado the following day to ski, so we went to check on her and see if we should stay home. She insisted we go on. She told us she wasn't worried about dying, and smiled as she said, *"You know how I like to travel."* Then she concluded, almost with a chuckle, ***"This time I don't even have to pack my bags!"***

We left content that she was O.K., but returned about 3:00 a.m. after receiving a call informing us Mom had died.

She was a small lady, about 85 pounds. As she lay there I thought, "I came from this tiny old woman." How grateful I was. She raised us to know the Lord; released us to become men; quietly stayed in our lives, but never tried to tell us how to live; always supportive; never condemning; growing in her faith all her life.

I bent down and kissed her to say, "Goodbye!" Dad died days before Jesus birthday. Mom died the day after, 28 years later.

She was at peace. This time, so was I!

From Grandpa With Love

Dear friends, I urge you as aliens and strangers in the world, to abstain from sinful desires, which war against your soul.

(1 Peter 2:11)

A Time to Receive—and Use God's Gifts

Age 44-60

58 *"Aliens and strangers in the world"*

The improvement in our physical well-being is evident, particularly since the Industrial Revolution. The problem seems to be the nature of man. Adam and Eve disobeyed God in the Garden of Eden. Cain killed Abel and we are still at it. No matter how hard we try, we just can't make this world right.

When a whole area of the world becomes affluent and things get better physically, the fire of the faith seems to die out (e.g. Europe and now the USA). Ultimately, we find a way to kill 70-80 million as in WWII and start over again. I count nine wars since WWII; now we can probably figure a way to kill billions of us!

Jesus repeatedly told us He was bringing in a *new* Kingdom (e.g. the Lord's Prayer) rather than giving us the task of fixing the physical Kingdom of the World, which will finally be replaced.

I believe we become citizens of His *new* Kingdom when we are "born again" into His Family and His Kingdom. But, that makes us *"Aliens and strangers in the world"*, (1 Peter 2:11) which can be very uncomfortable and cause us to feel out of step.

We continue to do "good works" but for a different reason. We try to let Him use us to reflect His Will and His Love here in this world—not to make this temporary Kingdom of the World better, but to be faithful citizens who love and attract others to His perfect, new and eternal Kingdom of God.

And it also often makes things better for those around us!

From Grandpa With Love

Life as a 24 Hour Day

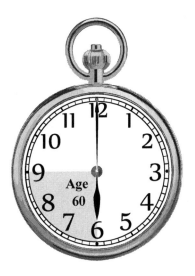

By Age 60 it is 6:00 p.m.
and
We are Tired and our "Day" is Winding Down

A Time to Harvest—And Pass It On
Age 60-70
(1985-1995)

He who listens to a life-giving rebuke

will be at home among the wise.

(Proverbs 15:31)

A Time to Harvest—and Pass It On

Age 60-70

59 *"Don't work too long."*

Not long before I retired, an older physician advised me, ***"Don't work too long."*** He then told me of an older surgeon who wanted to work as long as possible, but was concerned about making an error in his closing years. So he asked his long-time assistant to tell him if she saw evidence it was time. Finally, the assistant, (reluctantly, I'm sure), did as instructed. My friend then asked, "Do you know what her boss did?"—"He fired her!" He then concluded, "The point is, none of us think it's time for us!"

I have heard some caution, "Don't retire, or you will stagnate and die." For me, the stress of travel, competition and conflict made me more concerned I might die if I didn't retire! In fact, I believe I grew healthier and felt better after I retired than at age 65 when I began to make the change!

I do not know when is the right time, if ever, for you to retire. Samuel was probably about sixty-five years old when he gave up his position as Judge over Israel. Moses was eighty when he began to lead the Israelites out of Egypt, but he noted a normal life span of seventy to eighty years in Psalm 90.

I have concluded God has a way of telling us, if we will listen. We don't stop working. We merely change chapters in order to move on to the rest of the life and work God has for us in our later years. And it may have more lasting value than the earlier years.

I never regretted the decision. In fact, I shudder to think what I would have missed if I hadn't let go and trusted Him for the new!

From Grandpa With Love

Now the body is not made up of one part but of many.

****

If they were all one part, where would the body be?

(1 Corinthians 12:14; 19)

A Time to Harvest—and Pass It On

Age 60-70

60 *"I'm not your man, Grandpa!"*

Many of us have dreams of our children and/or grandchildren following in our footsteps. One of my grandsons taught me it doesn't always work out. He was probably around nine or ten years old and I decided it was time to introduce him to my world.

He followed me through our Law Offices, and I briefly explained the functions of various staff members. He seemed quite absorbed in our conversation, and I was thinking to myself, "He is really getting something out of this." I was feeling even better as he followed me out of one of the offices and called to me, "Grandpa". But he burst my grandfatherly bubble when he added, "Your belt isn't in one of the loops on your pants!"

It wasn't much of a start, but I thought it might go better if we actually had him play the part of the lawyer and I would be a pretend client. I told him, "You sit there behind my desk and I will sit here in front." I explained to him why I had come to him: "I have a car I would like to sell and I want you to draw up a contract of sale." I added, "How much will you charge me?

"How much is the car going to sell for?" he inquired. I was impressed and quoted him an amount—about $500, as I remember. He quickly responded with his proposed fee, "$500!"

I decided it was time to ask him if he wanted to be a lawyer. I never forgot his answer: *"I'm not your man, Grandpa!"*

I learned I can't make my children or grandchildren into me. But I can help them find who *they* are and blow wind into *their* sails!

From Grandpa With Love

Then you will have success if you are careful to observe the decrees and laws that the Lord gave Moses for Israel. Be strong and courageous. Do not be afraid or discouraged.

(1 Chronicles 22:13)

A Time to Harvest—and Pass It On

Age 60-70

61 *"What is your definition of success?"*

One evening an older woman gave me two very provocative questions. The first was, *"What is your definition of success?"*

At some point, she said, our definition will become our goal and dramatically affect our life. After much reflection, mine finally became a simple statement: "That I might be used by God to be and do what He had planned for me". It has nothing to do with my bank account, organizations, degrees, or offices. Rather, "Am I about the work God had planned for me?" If so, I think I'm successful; if not I need to change.

We were all created for a purpose, but we sometimes fall into a trap that becomes a substitute for the real thing.

One trap is to seek success in the eyes of the world. A second is our drive for success in one area may contribute to our failure in another. The divorce courts are grim recorders of many who become so intense trying to succeed in their careers that their marriages fail. A third very subtle trap is called altruistic egoism: I do good work for you, but my underlying goal is to reward me with money, reputation or other personal benefits.

I have concluded real success is to be involved in building God's Kingdom for God's glory without regard to our personal benefit. We do our work out of gratitude, because He has already saved us, and we want to bless Him with our lives. When we do, we get to share in *His* work.

That's *real* success!

From Grandpa With Love

When you find honey, eat just enough—

too much of it, and you will vomit.

(Proverbs 25:16)

A Time to Harvest—and Pass It On

Age 60-70

62 *"How much is enough?"*

I mentioned earlier two provocative questions I was asked by a friend's mother at a dinner party we were attending. We discussed the first question in the last One-Liner. But the second question was very timely as I was entering my sixties and wondering about my future. The woman and her husband were in their eighties, so I listened attentively. "Another decision you must make in life," I was told, is *"How much is enough?"*

How much money? How much house? How many children? How much work? How much travel? How much is enough—of everything? As I thought about the issue I determined there were some areas about my law work where I now had enough. I made the following decisions—and I never regretted them.

No More Trial Work. This is a game for young men or old lions. I decided I was neither. *No More Firm Management.* Those who are following cannot take their rightful place of leadership until we get out of the way. *No More Acquisition of Capital.* I decided that trading any more of my life for extra money wasn't a wise exchange. *Setting A Time Table.* I announced to my partners, that at age sixty-five I would sell my interest in the firm and go "of counsel", and I would retire at age seventy.

I do not know what decision you will or should make at your stage of life. But I do believe we should review our lives periodically and ask ourselves the question,

"How much is enough?"

From Grandpa With Love

I have given them the glory that you gave me,

that they may be one as we are one: I in them and you in me.

May they be brought to complete unity to let the world know

that you sent me and have loved them even as you have loved me.

(John 17:22-23)

A Time to Harvest—and Pass It On

Age 60-70

63 *"Complete—Don't Compete!"*

God gave us a heart to compete. But a quick survey of my Bible revealed a startling fact: the words "competition" and "winner" do not even appear in these scriptures, and related terms such as "compete, win, wins and winners" appear less than 25 times!

So I asked myself, "Against whom am I to compete, and for what?" I decided He wants me to fight—but not against others. Instead, I am to compete against Satan and evil for God's Glory and for the benefit of His Kingdom and other people.

The Apostle John's record of Jesus's final discussion with His disciples makes it clear He wanted *oneness*, not *competition*, among his followers. This seemed especially applicable to the relationships in marriage.

As my wife Ellie and I struggled through the early years of marriage, we found that husbands and wives are to *complete*, rather than *compete* with each other as the *two become one*. We worked through the Biblical roles of Husband and Wife, and I wrote our conclusions in *"Complete—Don't Compete!"* Gradually, I began to see it is also true in *all* of life: in our churches, our work world and community as well as our homes.

When we give up the battle to be *first* or to have the *most* or to be the *best*, we may not become *great* in the temporary Kingdom of the World.

But we surely do gain an indescribable peace and contentment in the eternal Kingdom of God that far outweighs the cost!

From Grandpa With Love

A new command I give you:
Love one another. As I have loved you,
so you must love one another.

(John 13:34)

A Time to Harvest—and Pass It On

Age 60-70

64 *"Your assignment for the rest of your life
is simply to love people, and to love me."*

Much has been written and discussed about the unrealized potential of healthy retirees who have time to help others as unpaid volunteers. However, it seems most of us will major in retirement doing what was a minor during our working lives. In essence, our avocation before retirement often becomes our vocation after retirement, whether it's working with our investments, teaching Bible studies, or playing golf. We don't seem to change to something new, as much as we expand what we were already doing.

My reassignment came shortly before my 65th birthday. After many months of asking directions, I was awakened early one morning with a sense of peace and a voice saying,

*"Your assignment for the rest of your life
is simply to love people, and to love me."*

When I asked, it was repeated. I was overwhelmed with the simplicity of it. So basic!

I know the Bible, through such scriptures as the Great Commandment and the Ten Commandments, always put God first and man second. But the order was reversed for me, perhaps because it was easier to love a perfect God whom I have not seen, rather than imperfect people, with whom I live and work and live.

I guess I wanted to do something *great for God*. Instead, God wanted to do something *really great through me!*

From Grandpa With Love

145

When Peter saw him, he asked, "Lord, what about him?"
Jesus answered,
"....what is that to you? You must follow me."
(John 21:21-22)

A Time to Harvest—and Pass It On

Age 60-70

65 *"What is that to you? You must follow me."*

Institutions are necessary, but they aren't perfect. If we don't participate in them we have to live isolated lives. If we do join in, they often ask (and sometimes require) us to submit to what they believe. As a result many of us have a running battle with our need to participate and the desire to stay true to our own convictions.

As the years progressed, one of my favorite institutions gradually became more and more liberal. I tried to solve the dilemma by being a member but not accepting any more leadership roles. It came to a head when I was asked to serve on the governing board.

I knew I was in the minority about their direction and I struggled between loyalty to the group and following my own principles. When the last evening came for making my decision I decided to walk and pray until God gave me the answer. When no light came, I told myself (and the Lord) I would recite scriptures I had committed to memory and trust Him to give me the direction I should go.

God finally gave me my answer as I recalled Peter's discussion with Jesus at the Sea of Galilee after His resurrection. Three times Peter was asked if he loved Jesus. Each time he answered in the affirmative and received marching orders. Then Peter turned from his own responsibilities and asked Jesus about the Apostle John.

I knew immediately Jesus' answer to Peter was my answer, too!

Jesus simply said, *"What is that to you? You must follow me."*

From Grandpa With Love

There is neither Jew nor Greek, slave nor free, male nor female, for you are all one in Christ.

(Galatians 3:28)

A Time to Harvest—and Pass It On

Age 60-70

66 *"You always were more of a Person than a Lawyer!"*

When we are young we often daydream about what we will be when we "grow up". We study and work to become useful and to achieve status and recognition. My avenue was the practice of law.

First, came an undergraduate degree, then a law degree and finally our bar exams. Learning we had passed and being officially sworn in was an exhilarating experience! After years of work we were lawyers! We announced it to all the world by the words on the entrance to the office and by the certificate hung on the wall.

As the years rolled by it became a part of me. Or, perhaps, I became a part of the law. Sometimes it was difficult to sort out who I was from what I did.

That all changed after I accepted Jesus as divine, and pledged to give God all of myself I was able. It gradually became clear the law was good and necessary to keep order in this world—but it wasn't going to go with me into eternity. There we will have new resurrection bodies and a new Kingdom. Being a lawyer (or a doctor, businessman, educator or any other earthly occupation) won't count. There will be no certificates in Heaven announcing our accomplishments.

It stroked my ego when someone introduced me as a lawyer. But I will always be grateful to one man who helped me recognize what was eternally important, when he looked at me and said candidly, *"You always were more of a Person than a Lawyer!"*

From Grandpa With Love

149

Hear my words, you wise men; listen to me, you men of learning.

For the ear tests words as the tongue tastes food.

Let us discern for ourselves what is right;

let us learn together what is good.

(Job 34:2-4)

A Time to Harvest—and Pass It On

Age 60-70

67 *"Describe my shoe"*

Life is a learning experience. Many of my lessons came from our children—some while they were young, but many of the best and most lasting teachings came after they were grown with expertise and experiences I had never known. Here is one example.

Our eldest son spent much of his adult life conducting Bible study groups in Israel and other areas of the Mideast. I learned a lot as we traveled together and talked about various Biblical issues. But he surprised me one day by declaring, "You think like a Greek."

When I inquired what he meant, His response forever changed my view of the Biblical world. *"Describe my shoe"*, he said. Somewhat puzzled, I looked down and told him what I saw: "It is brown, leather, somewhat used, turned up a bit at the toe and about ten or twelve inches long." "See", he responded, "you think like a Greek." Then he added the punch line: "Those in the Western world think in terms of *form*. A person from the Mideast would have told me, 'It's for walking'. They think in terms of *function*."

My view of the Bible, and how to study it, were never the same again. That conversation was the beginning of a series of eye-openers as we began to look at the Bible from the writer's perspective and their time and place. Many of my long held views changed. Some dramatically!

How grateful I am that we can learn from our children—if we will listen. Even when they say, *"Describe my shoe"*.

From Grandpa With Love

You turn things upside down,
as if the potter were thought to be like the clay!

(Isaiah 29:16a)

A Time to Harvest—and Pass It On

Age 60-70

68 *"Turn the world right side up!"*

After I decided to follow Jesus, it didn't take long to realize that the teachings of Jesus and the Bible often seemed upside down from the ways of the world.

As I read through the New Testament one year, I decided to test the concept by drawing upside-down stick figures where the Bible's teachings were opposite to our everyday world. The conclusion was obvious as the upside-down stick figures gradually sprinkled across the pages.

I began to see there are two kingdoms: the temporary Kingdom of the World and the eternal Kingdom of God. And we don't understand God's Kingdom until we decide to follow and obey Him. Until then, going into the Bible is like walking into a house and the furniture is all on the ceiling. You say, "What a strange and crazy house! It's all upside down!" But one day, you surrender your life to Christ and are "born again". When you walk into this same house the next time, you realize that your feet are planted on the ceiling. God's gravity for you has now shifted from earth to Heaven. You suddenly realize the furniture wasn't upside down, you were!

This realization opened up a whole new life for me. It changed how I thought, understood the Bible and how I was to conduct myself. It made me realize it wasn't my responsibility to make the world right. Only the Lord can do that.

Instead, I am to pray that Jesus would *"Turn the world right side up!"*—and let Him use me while He does it!

From Grandpa With Love

And He said, "I tell you the truth,
unless you change and become like little children,
you will never enter the kingdom of heaven."
(Matthew 18:3)

A Time to Harvest—and Pass It On

Age 60-70

69 *"I wike you and I wuv you!"*

One of our little granddaughters often told us, *"I wike you and I wuv you!"* She understood early in life there was a difference. As she grew older, her words were, *"I like you and I love you"*, but the distinction remained the same.

Love is what we do; *like* is what we feel. When I *love* someone, it means giving myself up for them. If I *like* someone, simply the thought of them gives me pleasure.

It is important that we *like* i.e. take pleasure, in our spouse, and others in our lives. Sometimes because they make us smile or laugh; or because we experience a rush of good feelings when we see their face or hear their voice; or the way they walk or talk; or we witness a kindness they pour out on someone (perhaps me) who doesn't deserve it.

It is even more important that we *love* i.e. give ourselves up for our spouse—and others God brings into our lives. And it is rather interesting that when we *love* someone, we often find it makes us *like* them!

We found over the years it wasn't enough merely to feel good (*like)* or to act right (*love*) our spouse. We needed to say so.

As time went on we often told one another, *"I like you and I love you"*—and sometimes, *"I wike you and I wuv you!"*

It is amazing how good it made both of us feel!

From Grandpa With Love

155

When they saw the courage of Peter and John and realized that they were unschooled, ordinary men, they were astonished and they took note that these men had been with Jesus.

(Acts 4:13)

A Time to Harvest—and Pass It On

Age 60-70

70 *"You were elected—now be the President!"*

When I was a young man I thought it would be exhilarating to be in charge. As time went by, I discovered being in charge wasn't as much about privilege and prestige as about responsibility. I found I enjoyed working independently and advising others, but had no particular desire to direct them.

When the nominating committee of our local service club came to me and wanted me to be President, I was dubious. I wasn't sure I was suited for the task. Maybe I just didn't want the responsibility. I thought about it and discussed it with my wife who encouraged me to accept. I finally did.

It was our custom for Past Presidents to meet with each incoming President and encourage and offer observations from their time in office and pass on any helpful hints. One man gave me the best advice when he said firmly and forcefully, *"You were elected— now be the President!"*

William Halsey, a World War II Admiral, allegedly told a young man who wanted out of responsibility, *"There are no great men. Just great challenges which ordinary men, out of necessity, are forced by circumstance to meet"*.

I am glad I accepted the responsibility. There were a few bumps, but it became one of the great experiences of my life.

And I found it was O.K. for an "ordinary man" to be President!

From Grandpa With Love

Nevertheless, there will be no more gloom for those who were in distress. In the past he humbled the land of Zebulum and the land of Naphtali, but in the future he will honor Galilee of the Gentiles, by the way of the sea, along the Jordan—

(Isaiah 9:1)

A Time to Harvest—and Pass It On

Age 60-70

71 *"The Bible has real people, in real places, and real times."*

For many years, I viewed the Bible as a wonderful spiritual guide. It had memorable stories and eternal principles, but the people, events and places were not real to me. That all changed when our leader on a study trip to Israel, exclaimed forcefully, *"The Bible has real people, in real places, and real times."*

The key that opened my interest was a reference to the "Galilee of the Gentiles". He explained the area we know as Israel was a land bridge for three continents: Europe, Africa and Asia. This tiny area less than 75 miles East to West and 200 miles North to South, was centered as the hub of the known world. It was perfectly positioned to radiate God's message to all the earth as the trade routes crisscrossed through Israel for centuries.

Jesus taught around the Sea of Galilee and destined the area to become famous. People come here to view and to study as they await the final battle of Armageddon a few miles to the south and look forward to His second coming as King of Kings.

When the places in the Bible became real to me, it helped the people and the events also become real. And as they become real, the Bible –and Jesus' return—no longer seem so distant in time and space and reality.

Hopefully, many of you can visit the Holy Land during your lifetime. But if not, modern technology can make it almost as real. And it surely helps when the Bible becomes real and reliable—not just a nice group of platitudes to make us feel good.

From Grandpa With Love

There is a time for everything...
a time to plant and a time to uproot....
He has made everything beautiful in its time.

(Ecclesiastes 3:1a, 2b, 11a)

A Time to Harvest—and Pass It On

Age 60-70

#72 *"S. O. S."*

I thought it would be difficult to make the break from full-time law practice, so I wrote to a few friends who were also in their sixties. I explained this was an *"S.O.S."* for some "Sold-out Seniors for Christ" to encourage one another as we retired, semi-retired, or kept going full pace as the case might be.

Several responded and for about fifteen years we met weekly, using the Bible as our guide as we prayed and exchanged experiences. Some died and were replaced. By the time we were in our late 70s and early 80's, I spoke with the men and it became clear it was time to disband. Here is part of my final letter:

"As I talked with you, it became apparent that we all enjoyed the fellowship, but the reason for getting together no longer has the importance and urgency that it once had—and that other things have become more important and need our time and attention..

It seems, therefore, that it is time to "be wise" and put "S.O.S." in our memory book. It has been "beautiful in its time", but it always seems a shame to hang on to something good too long and spoil it by trying to make it outlive its purpose."

As the years have progressed, I have become increasingly aware how essential it is that we have fellowship, particularly in the difficult transitions of life. There is a time to call for help and to walk through a chapter of life with some like-minded friends.

And there can also be a time to "let go" and move to the next chapter!

From Grandpa With Love

161

Then I heard the voice of the Lord saying,
"Whom shall I send? And who will go for us?"
And I said, "Here am I. Send me!"

(Isaiah 6:8)

A Time to Harvest—and Pass It On

Age 60-70

#73 *"Our Call"*

For many years I did not sufficiently appreciate the difference between our vocation and our job or profession. The world interchanges these terms and so did I. Gradually, however, I began to see our vocation, or what I now often refer to as our "voca", as in "vocal", is actually *"Our Call"* from God.

Our job or profession is the way we financially support ourselves, but only *one* place where we carry out our calling. Thus, if I am called to bring *harmony,* then I do it not only in my job or profession, but also in my home, church and community. And what a joy it is to find God has equipped us perfectly for what He calls us to do. In fact, it is one way we know it is *"Our Call"*!

Our calling may change as we move through life. I don't think we abolish or abandon what we were doing as much as we build on it. Age, health or other factors may cause us to retire from our job or our profession, but not from our calling. We are still to be about God's business, in whatever way he calls us to speak or to serve, even though we may now be financially supported by pensions or savings rather than by salaries or other earned income.

And when we retire from the work world, we have the golden opportunity to build on our early years to complete the final work God has for us in these later years.

Like Peter, we don't stop being fishermen; but now we are often freed up to concentrate on being *"fishers of men"*, without having to concern ourselves with catching fish!

From Grandpa With Love

But the noble man makes noble plans,
and by noble deeds he stands.

(Isaiah 32:8)

A Time to Harvest—and Pass It On

Age 60-70

 # 74 "Go to something—not just from something."

Moving from the practice of law toward full retirement at age seventy, was a difficult time for me. I learned the danger of sweeping out the old, but not having my heart and mind filled with something new. I know now never to leave a vacuum. Having a direction for the future is critical, or the devil may move in with all sorts of doubts and dark thoughts as he did to me.

I believe God has a unique plan for all the days of our lives. But we have to reach for them. For us, the later years included building a new home, moving to a new church, teaching many years in a large Sunday School Class, and consolidating many of the writings I began in my mid-fifties.

One booklet I felt was particularly appropriate for our grandchildren, I placed in our lock-box with a personal note, for delivery to each one as they reached age twenty-one. Later I placed my writings into five volumes known as the *From Grandpa With Love* series, and gave hardbound copies to our children and grandchildren so they can be used by them and be available for future generations.

All this gave purpose and direction, and helped fill the vacuum.

I don't know each person's vision or late in life mission. It may not require a change of location or vocation.

But I believe it does help when we *"Go to something—not just from something."*

From Grandpa With Love

165

Even when I am old and gray, do not forsake me, O God,

till I declare your power to the next generation,

your might to all who are to come.

(Psalm 71:18)

A Time to Harvest—and Pass It On

Age 60-70

#75 *"Learn to manage deterioration."*

As I approached my 70th birthday, I decided it was time for me to visit with someone who had already lived through some of the years up ahead. I called a man I respected who was about 10 years my senior and we set the date.

I asked one of our teenage grandsons to go along, for the fellowship and also for what he might learn. I said, "Come on and you can learn what you need to know for your 70s." I had to smile at his honest reply, "But grandpa, I don't think I'll remember!"

We flew down to our host's city and met with him for two or three hours. He gave me several bits of advice that were helpful, including the admonition to concentrate on the core items of life: Health, Wealth, Relationships and Usefulness.

But the most impactful advice was his suggestion, ***"Learn to manage deterioration."*** He pointed out that most of our younger years have been spent managing *growth* in our families, our finances, our businesses, our churches and other institutions. It has been exciting to expand. Now we must learn the difficult art of *managing deterioration.*

As we concluded our talk, my 80+ year old mentor wrote his telephone number on a piece of paper, handed it to my grandson, saying, "Call me in 20 years and tell me how you're doing." Then he thought a moment and said, "Make that 10 years!"

Isn't it amazing how deeply we can be impacted for life by a two or three hour conversation with a wise older person!

From Grandpa With Love

To the Jews who had believed him, Jesus said,
"If you hold to my teaching, you really are my disciples.
Then you will know the truth, and the truth will set you free."

(John 8:31-32)

A Time to Harvest—and Pass It On

Age 60-70

76 *"Trying To Do Right"*

I believe most of us would say we are *"Trying To Do Right."* But in our fast-changing, pluralistic society, it often seems confused and unclear as to what "right" really is. As I looked back at life, I centered on three avenues: Law, Ethics, and Truth.

Abiding by the Law of a particular government or other institution may bring order and the approval of those in authority, and abiding by the Ethical code of our peers may bring us the approval of a majority of that particular group, but neither will assure we are doing "right". Doing "right" requires living by Truth.

Truth is reality. It is what is. It is an infinite and omniscient view of life and how it should be lived. Truth is perfect. It is eternal. It never changes. Truth is the same everywhere. It brings harmony and order. It does not bring about bad, but good.

Every individual and group must ultimately face their own moment of Truth. When I realized that there was no certainty in laws and standards of ethics which changed with the times, places and persons involved, I was deeply troubled. In desperation, I turned to Jesus and the Bible. There I found a reliable basis for all of life, including stable and enduring marriages and families; help in resolving disputes and avoiding litigation in an increasingly adversarial society; aid in choosing and enjoying a life work; and an eternal view of time and the chapters of life.

I pray you will seek and find the same eternal Truth!

From Grandpa With Love

So I turned my mind to understand, to investigate and to search

out wisdom and the scheme of things and to understand

the stupidity of wickedness and the madness of folly.

(Ecclesiastes 7:25)

A Time to Harvest—and Pass It On

Age 60-70

77 *"'Why' may be the most important question we ask!"*

Sometime ago a long-time friend and former client and I were discussing some of the deeper questions of faith. I mentioned how much my life had changed after I surrendered my will and accepted Jesus as divine. For me it had been like night and day.

"But, Marvin", he countered, "You always were a nice person", referring to my softer demeanor which I fear he had mistaken for goodness. "The issue," I responded, "is *'why'* we do we do what we do. In my early days, I did what I did in the work-world for me and mine and to *make a name for myself*." In essence, I was voicing the desire which has plagued mankind since they tried to build the Tower of Babel, at the dawn of recorded history.

It brought to mind a conversation with another client while I was still actively practicing law. He was one who helped me better understand, when he said, *"'Why' may be the most important question we ask!"*

There are *worldly* reasons and *eternal* reasons *why* we do what we do. I may strive to *"make a name for myself"*, here on earth, but I will die and my glory will die with me.

So I ask, "Shall I follow ancient Eve, get the 'apple' I want, but die eternally? Or shall I follow Jesus, and not seek pleasure, possessions, power and position here on earth—in exchange for *real* life here in this world—and for eternity?"

This seems to be the basic choice each of us must make in life.

From Grandpa With Love

Life as a 24 Hour Day

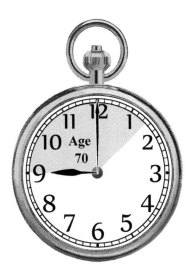

By Age 70 it is 9:00 p.m.
and
We Reflect on our "Day" and Some Fall Asleep

A Time to Get Ready —And Let Go
Age 70-85
(1995-2010)

...for I, the Lord your God, am a jealous God,
punishing the children for the sin of the fathers
to the third and fourth generation of those who hate me, but
showing love to a thousand generations of those who love me
and keep my commandments.

(Exodus 20: 5b-6)

A Time to Get Ready—And Let Go

Age 70-85

78 *"Four Generations: A Journey Through Life"*

As I approached age 70, I decided it was time to look back and prepare a family genealogy to pass on to my children and grandchildren. After working on the project awhile, it became apparent that I was acting as a reporter to discover and pass on third-hand information about people I did not know and events I had not witnessed—and that my children and grandchildren did not yet really know me! I determined, therefore, to first prepare and pass on to them an eyewitness account of my own 70-year span of our family history.

I attempted to set forth my life journey on paper and struggled to find a Biblical pattern to follow. The Bible often speaks of generations, particularly to the *"third and fourth generation"* (e.g. Exodus 20:5-6; 34:5-7), so we entitled it *"To the Fourth Generation"* and gave copies to our children at my 70th celebration.

During the next 20 years I added chapters for the 75th, 80th, and 85th birthdays. With the encouragement and help of several loyal friends, I finally prepared bound volumes entitled, *"Four Generations: A Journey Through Life"*, which we gave to all the children and grandchildren at my 90th Birthday Celebration. By then we had several great grandchildren—our fourth generation!

I asked my children to take their grandchildren for an hour while I spoke to my grandchildren. It was a once in a lifetime experience!

The tears and comments told me all I needed to know.

From Grandpa With Love

Then they said, "Come, let us build ourselves a city, with a tower that reaches to the heavens, so that we can make a name for ourselves and not be scattered over the face of the whole earth.

(Genesis 11:4)

A Time to Get Ready—And Let Go

Age 70-85

79 *"I think you just want your name on a book!"*

Writing has always attracted me. Even as a youngster, I was drawn to adventure stories, and later to histories, novels and all types of literature. Putting thoughts on paper seemed natural.

As a lawyer, I drafted contracts in the office and pleadings for the courts, including more complex briefs when cases were appealed. As I grew older, I wrote more and more personally about my faith and my journey with the Lord. Gradually, these took the form of booklets and small books.

Since the Tower of Babel (and before), mankind has been tempted to *"make a name for ourselves"*. I was no exception. I knew it was a potential problem, but I didn't know it was apparent to others. And I didn't realize it would be the backside of my gift and desire to write. That is, not until a good friend startled me one day by announcing, *"I think you just want your name on a book!"*

I decided to refute his claim by writing anonymously. But, after one booklet, I told myself, "This isn't fair. People are entitled to know who is writing so they can test their words by their life."

I finally hit on a compromise. My name had to go on the cover of books, but when I was writing small pieces, I put nothing but the titles on the covers, and placed my name inside in the copyright. Later, using the pen name, *From Grandpa With Love*, also helped.

I guess we never get over the temptations Satan throws at us. And we never get perfect solutions. But it does help to have friends love us enough to warn us—so we can *try* and change!

From Grandpa With Love

Children's children
are a crown to the aged...
(Proverbs 17:6a)

A Time to Get Ready—And Let Go

Age 70-85

80 *"From Grandpa With Love"*

The older I become, the more I am convinced that faith, family and friends are essential to life. And they are bound together by love.

In 1999, as we approached the new millennium, I was asked to speak with a group of college age students. I had some serious thoughts I wanted them to hear, but I also wanted them to know I was speaking in love. Since I was nearly 75 years old with grandchildren their age, I titled it *"From Grandpa With Love"*.

My children liked the title so well, they chose it for two large volumes of my writings they had bound and presented to me at my 80th birthday celebration. I was pleased they also felt it fit.

I understand Samuel Clemens adopted the words *"mark twain"* (the call used on river boat soundings for safe depths he heard in his years on the Mississippi river) as his pen name. *"From Grandpa With Love"* gradually became the same for me. As I walked through these older years, I enjoyed seeing it appear on my writings. It seemed to have a universal ring. It took the emphasis off me as a person, and let us all think as loving grandparents.

Recently, I overheard a discussion between an older couple that confirmed my decision. As they left a talk in which I used one of my writings, the wife asked her husband, "Why don't you write something like that?" He responded, "Why should I"?

And then he added wryly, "It is signed, *"From Grandpa With Love"*. And I am a Grandpa! "

From Grandpa With Love

179

In his heart a man plans his course,

but the Lord determines his steps.

(Proverbs 16:9)

A Time to Get Ready—And Let Go

Age 70-85

81 *"Just keep on doing it!"*

One of the most effective ministries I was privileged to enjoy is a para-church group called World Impact. They taught me much. One example was at a national meeting we were attending in California. The principal speaker was a nationally known author who had a heart for the inner city where World Impact was concentrating their work. His talk went something like this:

"You have asked me to come and give you some advice about working in the inner city. Actually, you are on the forefront of this work and others are watching and following you." Then he concluded, "Now, I know you don't know what you are doing. But my advice is, *'Just keep on doing it!'*"

His words have returned to me many times over the years. So often, I am in uncharted territory (at least, for me). When we start something new, it's hard to find a model. I hesitate and try and figure out what should come next. I talk with the Lord and sometimes with others. I don't know what I expect. Perhaps a clear sign from the Lord, like Gideon and his fleece. Or I am tempted to look for a modern day Urim and Thummim, like the Old Testament priests used in an effort to get direction.

Often, there are no direct answers. So I continue talking with Him and then move forward in faith one step at a time. Sometimes it unfolds and the road becomes clear. At other times I realize I still don't know what I am doing. But I know God does.

And since it seems to be working, I *"Just keep on doing it!"*

From Grandpa With Love

Now write another decree in the king's name
in behalf of the Jews as seems best to you,
and seal it with the king's signet ring –
for no document written in the king's name
and sealed with his ring can be revoked.

(Esther 8:8)

A Time to Get Ready—And Let Go

Age 70-85

82 *"Your copyright is, 'you have the right to copy'."*

Several years ago I stopped calling myself an *author*. Author comes from the word authority. I don't believe I am the authority when I write. Instead I like to use the word *writer*, to make it clear I am trying to convey what I believe God has given me to say. Hopefully, it will be clear *He* is the authority, and I am simply writing what God is putting on my mind and heart.

But this posed a dilemma. How was I to allow His message to move out to others, and still keep it intact and unchanged?

Over the years I struggled. I spoke with an attorney knowledgeable about copyright laws and the proper wording to insert. He gave me the standard version that usually appears at the beginning of virtually every published book. It kept the wording unchanged, but it also kept the message from going forward unless you *bought* our copy so *we* could make any money that might come from its distribution.

Since I felt the writings ought to be passed on without charge, we finally settled on wording that said in effect, *"You can reproduce this material, provided the copies are complete, including this copyright and circulated free of charge.".* He said it wasn't the usual language, but it worked.

As a retired lawyer, I know we have to use the right words if we want to be "legal". But, it would be refreshing if we could speak plainly and use the simple phrase one friend voiced to me:

"Your copyright is, 'you have the right to copy'."

From Grandpa With Love

And his gifts were that some should be apostles, some prophets, some evangelists, some pastors and teachers, to equip the saints for the work of ministry, for building up the body of Christ...

(Ephesians 4:11-12 (RSV))

A Time to Get Ready—And Let Go

Age 70-85

83 *"Don't ever say* **the** *minister!"*

There is a lot of lip-service about the ministry of the laity. But I found surprisingly few Christian professionals or members of the laity *really* accept that *all* Christians are called to be "*full-time*" ministers.

Several years ago, an older Christian pastor and author with whom I was visiting made the point with me very dramatically. I had come to visit him to discuss what my role should be after I tried to fully surrender my will and life to the Lord. During the conversation, I referred to my pastor as "*the* minister."

Forcefully pointing his finger at me, this elder statesman said sternly, *"Don't ever say* **the** *minister!"* And then he concluded, *"All* Christians are ministers!"

That is the clear teaching of Ephesians 4 in which it is stated that God has called some to be apostles, prophets, evangelists, pastors and teachers "*to equip the saints* (*all* believers) *for the work of ministry.*" (Ephesians 4:11-12 RSV)

Later, it was pointed out to me that less than 3 percent of Christians are professional "ministers" or "missionaries." Obviously, this number cannot reach the world for Christ. Instead, it is the task of all Christians to see themselves and all other believers as *ministers* and to recognize that it is through all such *ministers* that the world will be won for Jesus.

Not many are called to be *equipping* ministers. But we are all called to *minister.* I am so glad my old mentor set me straight!

From Grandpa With Love

185

Do nothing
out of selfish ambition or vain conceit,
but in humility
consider others better than yourselves.

(Philippians 2:3)

A Time to Get Ready—And Let Go

Age 70-85

84 *"But they took it away when he wore it!"*

People who love their work often find it difficult to retire. And so do people who have received recognition and status from their occupation.

We live in a world where credentials are often necessary to open doors and allow us best to do the work God has called us to do. However, I have found it is not wise to allow them to define us.

At times we are tempted to confuse our titles and type of work with who we really are. When that happens we may simply brandish *credentials* granted by Universities or other institutions to define us and assure others who we are. Many years ago an older mentor showed me a newspaper clipping to make the point. I have forgotten the names and titles, but the article went something like this: "Jay Thrakenberry, PhD, M.D., J.D., D.Min., will speak tonight. His subject is Humility!"

These marks of achievement are terribly important for some of us (including me) at times in our lives. Unfortunately, such recognition can build a sense of pride and superiority as we compare ourselves with others. When that happens we may get corrected in a way that can be embarrassing.

One man made the point with this little story: "A friend told me of a man who received a button for his humility." Then he added with a bit of humor in his eyes, ***"But they took it away when he wore it!"***

From Grandpa With Love

187

He has made everything beautiful in its time.
He has also set eternity in the hearts of men;
yet they cannot fathom what God has done
from beginning to end.

(Ecclesiastes 3:11)

A Time to Get Ready—And Let Go

Age 70-85

#85 *"Your work wasn't very important to you, was it?"*

Recently, one of our sons commented, in effect, *"Your work wasn't very important to you, was it?"* I was startled! I practiced law over 40 years and truly enjoyed it and thought it was worthwhile. But, after thinking a moment, I responded, *"No, as I look back at all of my life it wasn't that important."*

Later, I added, *"But, at the time it was very important. Looking back, the third grade is probably not very important to you, now. But when you were in the third grade it was the most important thing in life! That is the way my work was to me."*

Who we are and what we think and do changes as we go through life. Like going up a mountain, we see further the higher we climb.

At first we are so close to the foothills we can't see what is ahead, so we live in the *Present*. As we climb higher and have children of our own we begin to get a glimpse of a total *Lifetime*. Later, when we move into our fifties and have grandchildren, we expand our view beyond our own lifetime, and begin to think in terms of *History*. When we finally reach our last years and look out over our own history and the history of the world, many of us are captured by a fresh sense of *Eternity* and the *Kingdom of God*.

What is important at one level gradually pales as we see the work God has for us as we climb higher.

Best of all is realizing my most important work is to use my work, wherever I am on the mountain, to love people and to love God!

From Grandpa With Love

Go now, write it on a tablet for them,

inscribe it on a scroll,

that for days to come

it may be an everlasting witness.

(Isaiah 30:8)

A Time to Get Ready—And Let Go

Age 70-85

86 *"Writing is God's gift to an old man."*

Several years ago, an elderly Doctor who was writing his memoirs, told me, *"Writing is God's gift to an old man."*

But in a broader sense I have determined, *"Writing is God's gift to all mankind!"* Through writing we can receive from the past and give to the future.

The accumulated wisdom of the ages is available to us today because of the written word. What a gift! Not only does it overwhelm me with gratitude for what I can learn from earlier generations, it also challenges me to pass on all I can to help those who follow.

For me, the greatest and most profound writing is the Bible. Distilled in these pages is the Hope of eternity. It never grows old, and its breadth and depth are inexhaustible.

One of its great strengths has been the themes and common conclusions reached by various writers over thousands of years. For most of my life it has fed me and helped me see further, wider and deeper.

The Bible says we affect those who follow us to the *"third and fourth generation"* (and perhaps much further). What I do and say will, of course, have a lasting effect on those around me. And placing His lessons to me in writing may let them not only be read now, but also travel on to later generations, after I am gone.

I suppose that is one reason I keep on writing.

From Grandpa With Love

Always be prepared to give an answer to everyone who asks you to give the reason for the hope that you have.

But do this with gentleness and respect....

(1 Peter 3:15b)

A Time to Get Ready—And Let Go

Age 70-85

87 *"I'm so grateful that I know!"*

The following words were written in 1991 as part of an ending for the booklet, *"What Am I Missing?"* They seem increasingly important with each passing year, so I wanted to pass them on again.

Many years ago, I read with admiration the letter of a young man in his thirties who was approaching death by cancer. In this letter to his son, he carefully detailed qualities and observations which he encouraged his boy to consider and to emulate. What a wonderful legacy!

Recently, a long-time friend told me that he had learned he has only a few months to live. *"I'm so grateful that I know!"* he said, "I have always worried that I would die unexpectedly." At first, this seemed an unusual statement, but gradually I have seen the maturity of his wisdom as he was able to put his house in order before he passed away.

Unfortunately, not all of us will have the luxury of knowing *when* we will die. However, we all know in advance we *will* die, so we should act accordingly.

Last Wills and Testaments, Trusts, and Living Wills are obviously important considerations. But in a more narrow and personal way, so are the teachings of each of our lives. I encourage you, therefore, to consider your life and write down what has been important to you that you don't want later generations to miss.

From Grandpa With Love

The way of a fool seems right to him,

but a wise man listens to advice.

(Proverbs 12:15)

A Time to Get Ready—And Let Go

Age 70-85

88 *"We need to join that class!"*

After I retired, we decided to make some changes, including a new home and a new church. When we visited another congregation we had enjoyed over the years, some senior friends asked if I would teach a new class they wanted to form. Without praying or consulting Ellie, I curtly answered, "No! I think I am to work with younger folks." It was obvious they were shocked!

And so was Ellie! When we left, she told me quietly, but very emphatically and forcefully, *"We need to join that class!"*

I knew immediately I had messed up! As soon as we were home, I called the woman who had the vision for the class and asked if they would still have me. Now it was my turn to be humbled. "When I saw you in the service", she said, "I prayed and felt God tell me you were the man. I was so puzzled when you refused."

God taught me an invaluable lesson. It isn't my job to tell Him what I am to do. It is to ask—and listen for His answers. And to realize they may not come directly from Him, but rather from others He brings (sometimes unexpectedly) into our lives.

For me this ushered in a chapter of life that was a breath of fresh air. For nearly 15 years, I was blessed to study, teach and write what God was opening up to me, and pass it on to others who were hungry for his Word.

One of the best gifts God has given men is wives who now and then help us hear His voice and give us a message—such as, *"We need to join that class!"*

From Grandpa With Love

Brothers, stop thinking like children.
In regard to evil be infants, but in your thinking be adults.
(1 Corinthians 14:20)

A Time to Get Ready—And Let Go

Age 70-85

89 *"You are trying to get us to think!"*

I learned early in my law career that I could be a zealous advocate, but it was not a natural fit, and it hardened me. As time went on, I realized I enjoyed and was much more suited (and gifted) to search for, and find ways to resolve disputes and avoid litigation and to teach them to our clients and to others.

Later, as I was entering the world of the Bible I discovered it, too, was a "legal book". It is replete with words such as law, judge, judgment, witness, testimony, verdict, guilty, pardon, swear, oath, prison, sentence, govern, government, ruler, rule, inheritance, kingdom, etc.—and scriptures such as Psalm 19 and 119 in the Old Testament and the Sermon on the Mount in the New Testament both talk much about legal issues.

Working in the Bible was much like the work I had done in the secular Law books, and the part I enjoyed most was searching out issues and teaching and explaining them to others. I wanted to be sure they could understand, but I was primarily depending on the Holy Spirit to move them to act.

One Sunday morning, as I was explaining something I was attempting to get the class to *know*, I said emphatically, "I'm not trying to get you to *do* anything!"

A man stood up in the back row and responded just as emphatically. *"Yes you are.* **You are trying to get us to think!"** My answer was short and contrite: "I plead guilty!"

And, just think, I am still privileged to do it even as an old man!

From Grandpa With Love

...let the wise listen and add to their learning,
and let the discerning get guidance—

(Proverbs 1:5)

A Time to Get Ready—And Let Go

Age 70-85

#90 *"It's time to go to Larksfield!"*

Early in 2001 Ellie became aware that she was suffering memory loss. In the summer of 2005 she calmly announced, *"It's time to go to Larksfield!"* So we did.

We really enjoyed the next four years. She never tired of looking out our third floor window at the beauty of a sunrise or sunset as it spread across the sky and its rays flashed like fire from the cross atop the church we could see in the distance. Or watching a full moon and the city lights on the horizon. Often she would call me to share the moments with her.

Ellie left in September, 2009. Life was never the same. It was good to have the company of others close by, but it became increasingly clear we had moved for Ellie and I no longer fit. So, some of our children and I began to look for an alternative.

When I remarried in 2012, Jo and I decided to make a fresh start in a new location. It, too, was right for that period of our life. But four years later, our age and health told us our needs were changing. In early 2016, I told my wife, "I am 91 years old. Something is going to happen one of these days, and I don't want to leave you with a crisis."

It is exciting to change houses as our family grows, or we scale down in retirement. But we learned it is also wise to know what stage of life we are in, and go where we fit!

This time I was the one who calmly repeated the words, *"It's time to go to Larksfield!"*

From Grandpa With Love

199

There is a time for everything...
a time to be silent and a time to speak....
(Ecclesiastes 3:1a, 7b)

A Time to Get Ready—And Let Go

Age 70-85

91 *"Just keep your mouth shut!"*

I entered the Army Air Corps in 1943 at age 18, but it took so much time to train I only flew three missions against Japan, one of which happened to be the last mission of the war.

Now it was 70 years later and I was in my eighties, living in a Senior Center. One morning four of us, who happened to be veterans, were having breakfast together. The man sitting on my left was a friend of many years. The other two I had only known since moving to the Center.

The man across the table turned and asked me, "You were in the Air Force, weren't you?" I had heard he was, too, so I answered, "Yes. You were too, weren't you?" When he agreed, I asked what he had done. Without much emotion he replied, "I flew a B26 in Europe," and casually added a startlingly high (about 65 as I remember) number of missions.

The fellow next to him then spoke up, "I wanted to be in the Air Force, but I couldn't pass the physical." When we asked what happened, he told us, "Oh! They sent me over to an island in the Pacific." Then he described how he was blown out of a foxhole and sent home!

My friend, who had also been in the service but seen limited action like me, turned to me and whispered quietly:

*"When you're with guys like these—**Just keep your mouth shut!**"*

From Grandpa With Love

There is a time for everything...
A time to be born and a time to die.
He has made everything beautiful in its time.

(Ecclesiastes 3:1a, 2a, 11a)

A Time to Get Ready—And Let Go

Age 70-85

 # 92 *"Grandma was with me when I was born.*
I am with Grandma when she died."

My wife Ellie died on September 2, 2009, at age 82. The end came rather swiftly from a throat malfunction that kept her from drinking or eating. She had made it clear she did not want feeding tubes or heroic measures, so she went naturally and quietly.

These final days changed us as individuals and as a family. By being with Ellie as she finished her race, we deepened our relationship with each other and with God. I would not trade those days and hours and moments for anything in the world. Never was she alone. Always someone was there, loving her. And what a joy it was—because she had loved every one of us!

Ellie's middle name was Ruth. She was at our daughter's bedside when she gave birth to a little girl who was given the middle name of Ruth, in honor of Ellie. In the stillness after Ellie's final breath, this granddaughter, now grown up and married, said quietly, *"Grandma was with me when I was born. I am with Grandma when she died."*

Life is a continuum. It doesn't begin when we are born and it will not end when we die. God is doing something in history and He has allowed us to be in on it.

Death is as natural as birth. Ecclesiastes 3 tells us both are *"beautiful"* in their *"time"*. I believe we rob ourselves and future generations if we do not participate with our loved ones in this great moment of transition from the visible Kingdom of the World to the invisible Kingdom of God.

From Grandpa With Love

I tell you the truth, unless a kernel of wheat
falls to the ground and dies, it remains a single seed.
But if it dies, it produces many seeds.

(John 12:24)

A Time to Get Ready—And Let Go

Age 70-85

93 *"Letting go"*

"Letting go" has been one of the most difficult issues in my life. For years I struggled with wanting to be in charge, but God didn't allow me to fully understand it until Ellie died at age 82. I was 84.

It really began 40 years earlier when I *let go* of my will and gave God control of my life. Next was to *let go* of my wife Ellie and our children. As the years rolled by, I gradually *let go* of my law practice, heaping up money, and making a name for myself. Later, it was the right to be loved, thanked, honored, served, forgiven or comforted. Hardest and most poignant were in later years as I *let go* of Ellie and old friends as they left for Home.

Each decision felt as if I were losing a part of myself. But as the drumbeat rolled on, something unexpected happened: I stopped wanting what I thought would give me success and status in life, and God kept supplying me with all I needed. Instead of being poorer, each *"Letting go"* made me richer and more blessed!

I find no role in the Bible for great grandparents. Our first great grandchild came when I was age 79. On my 80th Birthday I announced (to non-one's surprise) I was no longer in charge.

By age 85, Ellie was gone, and I had little responsibility in any of the four earthly institutions of Family, Church, Workplace or Government. I felt at peace and ready to rejoin Ellie.

The principal game of life was completed. Now I was ready for "Overtime". But to my shock and surprise this would prove to be a *New Adventure* I never, in my wildest dreams, ever imagined!

From Grandpa With Love

205

Life as a 24 Hour Day

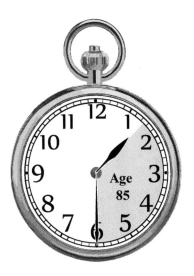

By Age 85 it is 1:30 a.m. the Next Day
and
The House is Quiet and We Soon Will Be, Too

Overtime!
Age 85-On
(2010-On)

Neither do men pour new wine into old wineskins.
If they do, the skins will burst, the wine will run out
and the wineskins will be ruined.
No, they pour new wine into new wineskins,
and both are preserved.

(Matthew 9:17)

Overtime!

Age 85-Onward

94 *"Thanks for the Adventure. Now go have a new one."*

Ellie, my dear wife of 61 years, went Home on September 2, 2009. She was the light and love of my life and it was a wrenching experience.   But it was God's will, and neither of us ever questioned it was the right time for her. We wouldn't have wanted it any other way.

However, it did leave me in a quandary. I knew it was to be a new life, but I didn't know just what to do. When I asked for direction, I seemed to get the same answer He so often offers those who are searching: *"You must follow me."* (John 21:22)

My dilemma came to a head after Ellie had been gone about a year and a half. Here is how I described the result in my journal:

I was given the DVD, "UP", an animated movie. Showing a couple of kids growing up, marrying and growing old together. They started with an "Adventure Book" with blank pages showing what they were going to do. Finally she dies. As an old, sad man, he opens the book and then realizes she had put in pictures of their life together. At the end of the last page was a note he hadn't seen before. She had written: 'Thanks for the Adventure. Now go have a new one.'   Love, Ellie.

I .... asked is this your word, and Ellie's word to me—to go forward and do whatever you have yet for me to do. To reach out? To risk more? To love and to live?... Dear Father, Show me now Your way and Your Adventure until you bring me home."

My answer came a few months later and it was a total surprise!

From Grandpa With Love

The Lord God said, "It is not good for the man to be alone.
I will make a helper suitable for him.

(Genesis 2:18)

Overtime!

Age 85-Onward

95 *"Would you come and do your recent seminar on 'The Last Half of Life'?"*

A few months after I saw the *Up* movie mentioned in the last One-Liner, a leader of my old church called and asked, *"Would you come and do your recent seminar on 'The Last Half of Life'?"* I still had many friends there, and I was honored to have the opportunity to share some of my journey with them.

The seminar was given on Wednesday nights following a weekly church supper. Two wives of deceased friends and I began to eat and then go to the seminar together. The next thing I knew the weekly dinners turned into other times with Joan, and we both were suddenly aware we were attracted to each other in a totally new way. We had been family friends for over 30 years, but this was different! A short time later, we decided to remarry.

We have had sign after sign that we are in God's will. But others were concerned. I found it is great for those on the periphery, but sometimes disconcerting for those who are closest to us. When we discussed it with others who had remarried they told us about similar experiences. This was confirmed by a young pastor who counseled children faced with similar new family dynamics.

One younger person thought it was *"weird"*. (And from their viewpoint it probably was!) An older widow quipped that she didn't want to be a *"nurse or a purse"*.

But neither of us ever had doubts. The seminar went well—and so has the marriage. I'm so glad I said *"Yes"* to both!

From Grandpa With Love

Then Moses entered the cloud as he went up on the mountain. And he stayed on the mountain forty days and forty nights.

(Exodus 24:18)

****

...and he (Jesus) *was in the desert forty days, being tempted by Satan.*

(Mark 1:13a)

Overtime!

Age 85-Onward

96 *"Forty days in the wilderness!"*

On June 21, 2012, my new wife and I left for Colorado. We were headed for a mountain home built by her and her former husband.

I couldn't shake the feeling I was going with *his* wife, in *his* 4 wheel vehicle, to *his* cabin, in *his* town, to be with *his* friends. I found *his* presence everywhere—*his* pictures, *his* carvings, *his* fishing gear, *his* hats, and *his* tools. I missed *my* people, *my* possessions and *my* position. I was nobody with nothing!

My wife sensed how miserable I was and offered to go home, but I told her I felt it was important that we stay through the summer. It finally became clear it was a time for me to voluntarily let go of everything, so God could start me with a fresh new slate. A tiny version of Moses' and Jesus', *"Forty days in the wilderness!"*

40 days after we left Wichita we both awoke to the realization God was stripping me of everything but Himself. He was teaching me *humility!* Over the next few days I recounted with joy and wonder the nearly endless good things that God substituted: mountains and drives; streams and walks; cool and rain; bucks, does and fawns in our yard; small town life and a mountain city charm with wooden boardwalks, shops and churches; Bible Studies; my 87th Birthday and a local artist to paint our WWII plane. The greatest joy of all, were the people, who were now my friends, too!

It was good to know Jo's past, but we never went back. We knew we couldn't recreate her old life. God had given us something new and it was time, *now*, to build *our* marriage and our *memories!*

From Grandpa With Love

I thought, "Age should speak;
advanced years should teach wisdom."
But it is the spirit in a man, the breath of the Almighty,
that gives him understanding.

(Job 32:7-8)

Overtime!

Age 85-Onward

97 *"Marvin, you are old!"*

As the years roll by, our age becomes increasingly important and obvious. But my aging took one of our younger friends by surprise. He approached me after a talk I gave in my eighties, and burst out, *"Marvin, you are old!"* I sensed it was a realization, not a condemnation. I smiled and answered, "Yes—and, it's O.K., isn't it? Young isn't good. Old isn't bad. They simply are!"

Every age has its own benefits and difficulties. Because we are so active when we are younger, age isn't on everyone's mind. But when there are only a few years left, it draws increasing attention. We now have limited time, mobility, ability and importance to the world. When I told one of our sons that I heard old folks become "invisible", he replied, "No Dad, you're irrelevant!" Not to loved ones or the Lord, but to the world. I responded, "Yes, and the world is becoming increasingly irrelevant to me!"

As I enter my nineties, I feel we are in a satellite, still bound by earth's gravity but circling the globe far above the clouds. The view is magnificent! Hills and valleys and streams increasingly fit together. And our new function and contribution is the wonderful privilege of telling those still down below what we see!

Only from this altitude can we begin to comprehend what old King Solomon concluded in Ecclesiastes. Repeatedly, he tells us that all his pleasures and possessions and position in the world were *"meaningless"*. Nothing more than *"chasing the wind"*!

So, don't feel sorry for us (or for you) when we are old!

From Grandpa With Love

Then King David went in and sat before the Lord, and he said,
"Who am I, Oh Sovereign Lord, and what is my family,
that you have brought us this far?"

(2 Samuel 7:18)

Overtime!

Age 85-Onward

98 *"Will the real Marvin Martin please stand up?"*

Once we surrender our will to God and receive and believe in Jesus, He begins to change us. And that can confuse us and those around us. So much so in my case that one of our children asked in frustration, *"Will the real Marvin Martin please stand up?"*

Early in life, we ask questions, experiment and take tests to help us determine who we are. Gradually we become aware we are a moving target. We are continually changing, sometimes gradually, and occasionally in a moment of crisis—but always changing. And we are changing, either more and more into what Jesus calls us to be, or drifting further and further from His Kingdom and His righteousness.

When we are younger we believe we will get it all figured out when we are older and we can stop searching because we will know just "Who I am", and "What I am to do."

Don't you believe it! I *am* old! And as I entered my 90's I found myself once again asking the question presented to me almost fifty years ago: *"Will the real Marvin Martin please stand up?"*

I know now, only God knows *the real Marvin Martin,* as well as the *real you and every other person who inhabits this world!*

And that is O.K. My job is just to keep seeking and following His directions until I go Home. Then I get to be One with Him and all the Saints.

The *real* challenge is to be sure I know and follow *Him!*

From Grandpa With Love

You will be his witness to all men
of what you have seen and heard.

(Acts 22:15)

Overtime!

Age 85-Onward

99 *"Dad, you never used to tell anything and now you tell everything!"*

I realize some folks may think it self-serving to relate events from my own life. Sometimes it becomes touchy because I describe personal events and the emotions they evoked. As one of our children said to me one day, ***"Dad, you never used to tell anything*** (particularly when I was a practicing lawyer with confidential information) *and now you tell everything!"*

But the older I became, the more I felt God's hand urging me to pass on what He gave me. It follows Jesus' statement to His disciples in Acts 1:8-9, *"But you will receive power when the Holy Spirit has come on you; and you will be my witnesses..."* This does not appear to be an option, but a fact or a command.

Not all of us can be *expert* witnesses who preach and teach, but I felt strongly I had no option but to be an *ordinary* witness telling others what I myself have seen and heard and experienced in my own life! Since ordinary witnesses are usually not allowed to give *"hearsay"* evidence in court, (i.e. what we *"hear others say"*), I concluded my job was simply to tell about experiences from my own life.

1 Thessalonians 5:21-22 tells us, *"Test everything. Hold onto the good. Avoid every kind of evil."* It caused me to place a note with many of my writings saying, in essence, *"We all err. So test what I say, hold onto what is good (of God) – and discard the rest."*

So.... enjoy what I say—but test it to see if it is really true!

From Grandpa With Love

Even though I walk through the valley of the shadow of death,
I will fear no evil, for you are with me;
your rod and your staff, they comfort me.

(Psalm 23:4)

Overtime!

Age 85-Onward

100 *"If they want to be with you!"*

I have never forgotten a crackling short wave radio broadcast in 1934 and a voice saying: "This is Admiral Richard E. Byrd from Antarctica!" Years later I read his book about his bleak time, alone, in that frozen wasteland. It was titled simply, *Alone!*

Years later I asked one of our daughters how we know if someone loves us. Her answer was simple: *"If they want to be with you!"*

God made it clear to Adam that "It *is not good for man to be alone"*. When Moses hesitated to go to Egypt, God said, *"I will be with you."* As Jesus left His disciples He assured them, *"I will come back and take you to be with me",* and He promised to send the Holy Spirit *"to be with you."*

Even as a young boy I knew others loved me *if they wanted to be with me.* As God and others loved me I found I wanted to love and *be with* others. And I found nothing beat Homecomings—after a War, a day at the office or Christmas time!

I received much from others in Boy Scouts, Air Force, Fraternity, Rotary, Church groups, informal gathering of friends, and meals and conversations with others who were hungry for God and people. It seemed not only natural, but commonsense, to practice law over 40 years with partners. And the highpoint was a lifetime of marriage, children, grandchildren and great grandchildren!

So, remember, when I leave: *"I'll look forward to seeing you in Heaven—because I love you and want to be with you!"*

From Grandpa With Love

221

We love because he first loved us....
And he has given us this command:
Whoever loves God must also love his brother.

(1 John 4:19; 21)

Overtime!

Age 85-Onward

101 *"All that is really important is loving and being loved."*

Some of my richest insights and memories have come from meeting with a small group of multi-generational men week after week for the past 30 plus years. The group gradually changes as some leave, some pass away and some are added.

When one of the old-timers recently reached age 90, a younger man asked him what advice he would give. Without hesitation he responded, "I've been thinking about that. I have determined, *"All that is really important in life is loving and being loved."*

We were shocked into silence for a moment. There were none of the usual debates or discussion. What he told us had been both simple and profound. And none of us wanted to argue or add to his conclusion.

I am age 93 now. I do not know what God has for these remaining years. But I do know He loves us. Sometimes His love seems to come direct from Him and sometimes through others He brings into our lives. And I know He wants us to receive, enjoy, increase and share all His gifts with others.

This will be the last One-Liner I intend to write in this series. It has been a great privilege to walk through these memories during the past 3 years. I have realized how much I owe to so many people who loved me enough to tell me what I needed to hear, even when it wasn't what I expected or sometimes probably wanted.

But I sure have learned a lot. And I hope you have, too.

From Grandpa With Love

Eternity

Looking Forward to Forever

This has been a book about *Time*: **Looking Back at Life**. Before we part, let's talk for a moment about *Eternity*: **Looking Forward to Forever.**

In the great chapter on *Time* in Ecclesiastes 3, the writer injects this frustrating oxymoron:

> *He has made everything beautiful in its time. He has also set eternity in the hearts of men; yet they cannot fathom what God has done from beginning to end.* (v11)

He doesn't make any further reference, nor try to explain *Eternity*. Probably because he can't! And neither can we! We know it exists, but our finite minds can only grasp the concept, not the reality of living for *Eternity* and dwelling in *Infinity*, where there is no time or space.

Life *has* been *"beautiful in its time."* Although the journey has been a series of ups and downs, highs and lows, happiness and tears, I would not have missed it for anything. But it will soon be time for me, like everything in this world, to leave. And that brings the Big Questions: What happens next? Where do we go? How do we spend *Eternity*?

Death is the haunting question in life. Were it not for the promises of the Bible I sense right now, at age 93, I would be experiencing panic and futility at the prospect of simply dying and returning to dust. For those who believe this is all there is, this is the Land of Life as we move toward Death. But for followers of Jesus, this is the Land of Death moving toward Eternal Life.

For me there is a great sense of Expectancy and Eternal Hope that far outweighs the beauty of this world and the temporary separation from the people I cherish and love. What lies ahead is so much grander and more meaningful and beautiful than my small finite mind can even grasp, that I am in awe. To spend *Eternity* in the Presence of God and the presence of all the people I love is simply overwhelming. Far beyond my ability to comprehend or even imagine!

I know now there is a *"time for everything"* and *"everything is beautiful in its time"*. But I also believe with all my heart and being that there is also an *Eternity*; and when *Time* here is over, a perfect *Eternity* with the Lord and all the Saints will go on forever. The beauty of this world will pale in comparison to what lies ahead, for those who are willing to die to themselves in this world and receive Jesus as the King of the Kingdom of God.

Because of all this I am more excited about the future than I have ever been in all my life!

See You in Heaven!

From Grandpa With Love

44152456R00130

Made in the USA
Middletown, DE
03 May 2019